O9-ABG-851

ELEPHANTS

Gentle Giants of Africa and Asia

Foreword by William Travers, ELEFRIENDS

Marcus Schneck

PORTLAND HOUSE

NEW YORK

Copyright Todtri Productions Limited d/b/a Book-Makers, Inc. 1991 All
rights reserved. No part of this publication may be reproduced, stored in
a retrieval system, transmitted, or used in any form or by any means,
electronic, mechanical, photocopying, recording or otherwise without the
prior permission of the copyright holder.

This 1991 edition published by Portland House, distributed by Outlet
Book Company, Inc., a Random House Company, 225 Park Avenue
South, New York, New York 10003.

This book was designed and produced by
Todtri Productions Limited
P.O. Box 20058
New York, NY 10023-1482

Printed and Bound in Singapore

Library of Congress Catalog Card Number 90-63252

ISBN 0-517-05690-9
8 7 6 5 4 3 2 1

Author: Marcus Schneck
Producer: Robert M. Tod
Designer and Art Director: Mark Weinberg
Editor: Mary Forsell
Typeset and Page Makeup: Strong Silent Type/NYC

TABLE OF CONTENTS

FOREWORD

Some people say that extinction is part of evolution—that we should allow the natural process of losing plant and animal species to run its course. So, should we say goodbye to the elephant, the largest land mammal left on earth?

From a strictly anthropocentric point of view, the answer must surely be yes. The elephant has a voracious appetite for both land and food. Elephant herds require vast areas in which to live—areas that are consequently denied to humans. A single elephant consumes up to three hundred pounds of food a day and can be difficult and temperamental, especially the African species. From a completely unsentimental point of view, the elephant is "useless." It may have symbolic significance in the fables and legends of the West and be associated with the afterlife in the East, but in practical terms—with the exception of some work done by Indian elephants— the elephant has no use in modern society.

Yet, in recent years, no other creature has inspired such a heartfelt surge of support and protection as the beleaguered elephant. People all over the world, from princes to politicians, scientists to sentimentalists, have rallied to the cause of the elephant in its hour of need.

With good reason. If we can step back a moment from our conventional view of the world that places us at the center, with all other life forms conscripted for our use and abuse, the elephant is certainly one species that can challenge our self-îappointed position as the supreme being on earth.

With a complex social society to rival our own—one based on love, understanding, compassion, remorse, and tolerance—elephants have long lived in harmony and balance with the plants and animals that share their environment.

Human beings, on the contrary, are driven by a desire to dominate, an insatiable greed for material wealth, and a rampant urge to procreate beyond the needs of survival or sanity. Consequently, as our influence and numbers have grown, we have forced the elephant into increasingly smaller spaces, denied it the freedom to search for and find enough food, and slaughtered it in hundreds of thousands for its tusks—its ivory—so that, when ultimately it is gone, we may perversely console ourselves with carved reminders of its passing.

If we can find it in our hearts to ensure that the world we live in has enough room for elephants, then there is hope for the rest of nature. By saving the elephant, we may give this amazing species, the rest of the natural world, and in passing, ourselves, a chance—there is still time.

I hope this book will be read as a celebration of the living elephant, that the pictures and text will evoke compassion and understanding for a nonhuman "tribe" of great, gray people that will continue to walk this earth with us.

William Travers,

Elefriends

INTRODUCTION

The rotting, gray-black carcass was covered with white streaks of excrement from the vultures and marabou storks that had been feasting on the massive kill. Half of the once-great head was all that remained. The face was completely missing. Hacked bone and flesh and brain protruded from the spot where the face should have been. Flies of a dozen different species buzzed around the mound of dead flesh by the hundreds. An all-pervasive stench filled the air, so thickly that it can be tasted.

This is an elephant after the poachers are through with it. They've gunned it down, hacked away its massive face in the hasty removal of its ivory tusks, and left the carcass to rot. Only the tusks—which might have weighed a few hundred pounds at most—of an animal that totaled several tons have any value to the poachers.

More than any other animal, the elephant has come to symbolize both the worst and the best that man has to offer his fellow travelers on this planet. We've hunted the great beast almost to the brink of extinction for no better reason than artistic ornamentation. But almost within sight of that precipitous edge from which there can be no return for all time, we've also responded to the plight of the animal on a worldwide level.

Certainly, other creatures have been pushed further than the elephant by man's designs. The passenger pigeon was wiped forever from the North American skies by market hunting that placed a value of only a couple of cents on each dead bird. The flightless dodo passed into oblivion by the seventeenth century, less than two hundred years after it was first identified on islands in the Indian Ocean by passing sailors who make a quick feast of the species.

Even today there are many species in far more dire circum stances than the elephant. The rhinoceros has been slaughtered for its prized horn to the point that there will probably be none surviving in the wild by the twenty-first century. Many of the big cats are also in peril. There may be no genetically pure red wolves left on earth today. And the list goes on and on, to a terrible extent.

But of all these creatures, the elephant emerges again and again as the symbol. Perhaps its great size and unique physical attributes play some part in this. Or, perhaps the long fascination that man has held toward the animal, dating to some of the early cave paintings, is

the reason. In the following pages, I attempt to explore these and other aspects of the venerable elephant.

THE ELEPHANT IN PERIL

Africa's elephant population has dropped from an estimated 1.3 million in 1979 to less than 610,000 today. Current estimates of the total population vary with the agency or organization making them, from less than 600,000 to nearly 800,000, but there seems to be greater agreement on the lower figure.

If the current rate of loss is not thwarted, it's entirely possible that the big animal will not exist in the wild by the turn of the century. According to the African Wildlife Foundation, "Scientists estimate that 90,000 elephants were killed by poachers in Africa [in 1989]. Another 10,000 [mostly orphaned calves] died as a direct result, bringing the total to 100,000. That's more than 270 a day...11 an hour...one every five-and-a-half minutes."

Beyond direct attacks by humans in search of ivory, elephants also occasionally fall victim to unintended poaching. Elephants sometimes chance upon metal snares that local peoples commonly set to capture other animals with which to supplement their diets. The pachyderm's natural curiosity leads it to examine the strange apparatus with its trunk. If it's unlucky, the elephant might get its trunk snagged in the snare and even lose part of it.

Asiatic elephants offer ivory poachers less reason to ply their bloody trade. Many males and practically all females never develop any tusks whatsoever. Nevertheless, the population of that species has fallen from as many as two hundred thousand at the turn of the century to less than fifty thousand today, with more than ten thousand of those animals living in captivity. Habitat loss to human uses is severe throughout this region, but poaching is the primary reason for the dwindling population.

Poachers are responsible for most of this decimation in Africa as well, although an exploding human population and the subsequent encroachment on wild spaces is also a factor. To illustrate by way of a drastic example, in Kenya—where poachers have been killing elephants at the rate of several per day—elephant numbers have declined from about sixty-five thousand to less than twenty thousand in ten years; human numbers have more than doubled there since 1970.

The space squeeze on the elephants will only continue to grow worse in the coming years. In the late 1400s and 1500s, when European nations were beginning to stake claims on the Dark Continent, there were an estimated ten million elephants and perhaps fifteen million people. The Global 2000 report foresees a total African population of well over eight hundred million people by the turn of the century, more than double the number that existed on the continent as recently as the mid-1970s. It takes a great deal of land converted from wilderness into agriculture to meet even the most basic dietary needs of eight hundred million people.

Even the continued existence of the wildlife reserves and national parks that Africa supports today cannot be taken for granted. Undoubtedly, some will be gone forever by the year 2000 and perhaps most will be substantially reduced in size. Areas considered safe havens for elephants today quite possibly will be something quite to the contrary tomorrow.

For many reasons, it is nearly impossible for elephants to coexist in areas where humans live in densities of more than three people per square mile. By 2000, agricultural expansion will have reduced such areas in Africa to a single-digit percentage of what once existed.

A particularly heartless impact of what in most recent years has been unchecked slaughter is a strange skewing of the population dynamics of most herds of elephants. The older bulls and cows— those individuals with the greatest ivory per animal— were killed off first. Then, with the world market for the precious material soaring to about 825 tons per year, the poachers turned their weapons on the younger elephants to meet the demand. These younger animals each carried less ivory than the mature individuals, and so the poachers killed more of them to maintain their supply. The average weight of a tusk imported into Asia dropped from almost thirty-six pounds to just ten pounds.

The Ivory Ban

On July 18, 1989, Kenyan President Daniel Arap Moi set five to twelve tons—three million dollars' worth—of tusks from elephants that poachers had shot but left behind to make their escapes. He did so to dramatize the drastic situation, call greater international attention to it, and push for severe international action to remedy it.

In October 1989, the Convention on International Trade in Endangered Species (CITES) made all trade in ivory illegal among its 103 member nations by moving the African elephant from its Appendix II list of threatened species to the Appendix I list of endangered species. (The Asiatic elephant has been listed on Appendix I for many years.) The ban, which actually went into effect in January 1990, appears to have struck successfully at one of the prime incentives for the poachers: Price is reported to have fallen from a high of more than one hundred dollars per pound to less than two dollars.

Such a drop in the price of their ill-gotten product is about the only language that really speaks to the poachers. In Kenya the annual per-capita income is less than three hundred dollars, and even the minuscule tusks of a few small elephants can earn more than that with just a few quick shots of an automatic assault rifle. Even the threat of being shot and killed on sight if caught by game wardens can seem small in the face of such potential gain.

At the same time, the ban seems to be hitting hard at the primary consumers of tusk ivory, the ivory-carving factories of Asia. A Worldwide Fund for Nature study found that in the wake of the ban many of these factories have shut down and others have dramatically cut back their workforces. Prices for their products were reported to have fallen as much as fifty percent, and dealers had been experiencing great difficulty meeting even a small percentage of sales in previous years.

Even the countries that had filed reservations to moving the African elephant onto the Appendix I list (and thus were not bound to end their trade in ivory) faced an extensively reduced market for their products. Large storerooms of carved ivory remained full, because the product did not have as extensive a market as it once did; factories that had once employed hundreds of people only had a handful of workers left.

As a precursor to the October 1989 action, the Ivory Trade Review Group issued a report in January 1989 calling for the Appendix I listing and an immediate end to all ivory trading. One month later, United States President George Bush made use of powers entrusted to him by Congress in the October 1988 African Elephant Conservation Act, and banned ivory imports from Somalia. He took that action after soldiers from Somalia were killed in Kenya in the act of poaching.

In June 1990 that United States ban was extended to include all ivory imports from all sources anywhere on earth, after several African nations, the World Wildlife Fund, and Wildlife Conservation International issued pleas for a total international ban on all ivory sales. Also in June 1990, the European Economic Community, as well as Japan and Hong Kong—the two primary markets for ivory— issued similar bans.

Some African nations, pointing to their own increasing elephant herds, have filed reservations to the Appendix I listing, meaning that they can continue to sell their ivory legally. These exemptions and reservations to the Appendix I listing may have led to a spate of slaughter by poachers trying to take advantage of remaining markets before they completely dried up. Kenyan officials reported that nearly sixty elephants had been shot in Tsavo National Park in the first two months after the CITES action. They blamed the motivation for the killings on Great Britain's decision to put off the ban until Hong Kong (a British colony) had cleared out existing stocks of previously carved items. The officials estimated that more than two thousand elephants had died across Africa during those same two months.

The international ban should, in theory, eliminate any international markets for ivory, even from those countries that filed reservations. But the action could also open the door for the poached ivory to move through those countries.

Poaching and Other Threats

The work of John Patton—a senior research associate in biology at Washington University, in St. Louis, Missouri—may eventually be of some help to law enforcement authorities in this regard. He is working to extend the emerging field of DNA fingerprinting and other genetic techniques to include the elephant.

Under a grant from Wildlife Conservation International, a division of the New York Zoological Society, Patton is developing a genetic database of tusks confiscated by African authorities. From these tusks he isolates samples of DNA, the genetic material in all cells that is often referred to as the "blueprint of life." He then searches these samples for chromosomal clues, or fingerprints, that might reveal genetic variation among elephants from different regions in Africa.

His goal is to use this information to pinpoint the type of elephant the tusks came from as well as the location on the continent of that elephant type. Using this information, authorities then can begin tracking the paper trail that will help them to regulate the trade in illegal ivory.

Tracking down ivory poachers has long been the bailiwick of African game wardens and local police, whose sleuthing techniques are timeworn and often inconclusive. Prior to the international ban on ivory sales, African countries set quotas on the number of elephant tusks allowed for sale or export. In some countries, hunting the animals is entirely illegal. But dealers got around these often-lax rules by selling their tusks through another country, often with the help of government officials willing to falsify papers.

In this way, some countries have become legalized conduits for poached ivory. Some have even exported more tusks in one year than they had elephants. Others without any elephants of their own still had an export quota. This created a very dirty paper trail, with authorities being able to point to their books and say they were falling within their quotas, even while ivory was being smuggled through their ports.

But Patton's genetic profiles will provide an analysis of tusk types that will be highly accurate, enhancing efforts to finger the culprits. The researcher describes the advancement offered by the DNA fingerprinting techniques as the "difference between searching the Empire State Building and just one room in the Empire State Building. We hope our genetic profiles will give authorities and scientists alike that one room."

However, the near total shutdown of the ivory markets—even if this is the lasting, long-term effects of the ban—by no means signals that the elephant is out of danger. Only when numbers begin to increase in many countries where they reside will the tide truly have turned. So many adults in their prime reproductive years, which is also the period when they carry the most ivory, have been killed in recent years that it could be several decades before such a widespread increase begins. Surveys in many regions of Africa fail to find any elephants older than thirty years of age, which is the time in life when many bulls begin breeding. In addition, researchers are discovering many family groups following matriarchs in their early twenties; a young age very this lead cow, which usually acts as the group's repository of all knowledge about the environment.

In addition, zoos cannot be relied upon as the last-ditch-effort repository of the elephants if the wild populations cannot recover. Few zoos have instituted breeding programs for elephants because obtain new stock from the wild has not been problematic, and the elephants they already have are extremely long-lived. Further, zoos tend not to include bull elephants because of the aggressive and difficult musth periods they undergo.

The Washington Park Zoo in Portland, Oregon, is a notable exception. More than two dozen Asiatic elephants have been born there in the past thirty years. Other zoos may join Washington Park as techniques of artificial insemination are perfected, eliminating the need for each zoo to maintain bulls in their collection. But such breeding programs are many years in the future, even under the best of circumstances.

And, the ban on ivory sales is a two-edged sword. Several African nations represented in CITES actually filed reservations to it because of the potential loss in revenues available for elephant protection and research that it was thought to represent. South Africa, for example—one of the few countries where elephant numbers have actually increased in recent years—was earning nearly two hundred thousand dollars per year from the sale of ivory gathered from elephants culled by government rangers to prevent overpopulation in Kruger National Park.

Although conservation groups from around the world are now pumping much-needed funding into the African game agencies' efforts to protect their elephants from poachers, this is a very recent development. Even now the protectors are undergunned, underequipped, undertrained, and underpaid. For example, a range might be expected to go up against poachers armed with AK-47 assault rifles, himself armed with a World War II vintage bolt-action rifle. At times, he might not even have ammunition for his weapon. Despite their severe disadvantage, rangers often wage fierce battles with the poachers. Many have forfeited their lives as a result. But no matter how many rangers are put in the field and how well equipped they are, the field efforts alone will never completely stop poaching. The areas to be protected are just too large, as are the underground organizations supporting the illegal activity.

Sadly, there have been repeated incidents in which the very people who were trusted with the protection of the elephants turned to poaching the animals to supplement salary that was low, when it was paid at all. Men with military connections within various African nations sometimes turned their weapons against the elephants in their own countries as well as neighboring lands.

In addition, there are those incidents that occur well beyond the realm of wildlife management that nevertheless have devastating impact on the animals. Many of man's wars in recent times have been fought in prime elephant habitats and have included the pachyderms among its victims. In Uganda, for example, the total elephant population has plummeted from nearly twenty thousand in the 1970s to less than two thousand today. The soldiers in dictator Idi Amin's armies were often permitted to decimate entire herds in a matter of minutes. Prior to the war in Vietnam, that country and neighboring Laos and Cambodia each had more than twenty thousand elephants. Today, less than two thousand roam those countries.

The impact of tourism is another unknown factor in the puzzle of whether wild elephants will exist in the twenty-first century. The day of the great white hunter is pretty much past, but the day of the great white nature lover with pockets deep enough to pay thousands of dollars to view African wildlife is really only dawning. These visitors represent millions of dollars in hard currency that most African nations need desperately. The questions that remain to be answered are how the money will be put to use and whether any of it will find its way to the peoples who live near the elephants and must contend with the incumbent problems.

Hunting and Culling

Although it has diminished, hunting is not entirely dead. Some African nations, notably South Africa, have incorporated sport hunting for animals that need to be culled into their management programs. This move brings in needed dollars from the sportsman, saves the governments money that would otherwise have been spent to pay government hunters to do the shooting, and gives the wildlife added value to the local landowners and economies. As a direct result, poaching has nosedived in South Africa.

Although we may not like the idea of even one more elephant being killed for any reason, there is some evidence to support the "conservation through utilization" approach of countries such as Zimbabwe. By way of example, the elephant population in Kenya, under strict no-harvest protection throughout the 1980s, dwindled from approximately sixty-five thousand animals to nineteen thousand in 1989. However, in Zimbabwe—where the inhabitants benefit from the animals both as a tourist attraction and a hunted species—grew from thirty thousand to more than forty-three thousand over the same period.

Similarly contrasting patterns are reported among the various African nations that side with one or the other of these approaches to managing their elephant herds. Observers have even forecast that the elephant will die out in some of the countries that follow the Kenyan model by early in the twenty-first century.

Of course, the full impact of the worldwide ivory ban must now be factored into the equation. This may exert a slowing influence on the loss of these countries' elephants. With less than a year under the ivory ban at this writing, it is much too early to assess the full impact of that action. Observers worry that ivory markets might simply move underground in response to the ban, something that could cause the price to actually rise in the long term.

Initial indications are promising, but similar bans have not had the desired effect on dwindling populations of other endangered species. For example, from the time of the 1976 ban to the present on black rhinoceros horns—which were sold in powdered form as an aphrodisiac—the world's total population of the animal has fallen from approximately fifty thousand to less than thirty-five hundred.

Also, poaching of elephants for meat is not likely to be impacted by the ivory ban. After three decades of war in various parts of Africa, high-powered weapons are commonly available at bargain-basement prices. Much of the problem in combating the poaching of elephants necessarily lies with the native peoples who live near the world's remaining herds. The altruistic motives of saving such a unique animal from oblivion is obviously lost on the farmer whose entire crop for the year has just been destroyed by a passing herd of elephants. Additionally, a single ivory tusk might represent more cash than an entire year's salary in nearly all of these Third World areas, when a job can be had. Sometimes, too, the financial gains of tourism are not returned, even in part, to the peoples of the areas that support the wildlife. All these factors can contribute to a less-than-enthusiastic response of local peoples to saving the elephant.

In southern India, there is even a ruthless elephant butcher who has gained an undeserved Robin Hood-like status with villagers. Veerappan, whose gangs reportedly have killed more than five hundred elephants for their ivory, as well as twenty men in the process, is the country's most wanted criminal. But efforts to stop his actions are hindered by villagers, to whom Veerappan is a benevolent employer. As many as four hundred people are said to work for him, and he regularly builds temples for and makes loans to these dirt-poor villages.

Culling, or cropping, is a government-sanctioned practice of removing elephants from the general population in overcrowded areas. The meat is given to the local peoples, the tusks and hide are sold, and some of the money returns into the local economy.

The biological reason for culling is to deal with overcrowded conditions for elephants. This is sometimes focused on entire family groups. In this way the strong interpersonal relationships that exist within other groups is not disrupted, according to official policy. Some researchers and observers, however, argue against any policy of culling, pointing out that the full relationships of the elephants to their environment and to the other wildlife inhabitants are not fully enough understood to justify such death-sentence pronouncements. The elephants' damage to the environment has been going on for many centuries and quite possibly is a needed impact.

This counterargument continues: The elephant's destruction of trees actually releases the nutrients held captive in the trees and helps convert them back into fresh raw material. On the broader scale, the elephants convert forest areas into open, grassland areas that eventually grow back into forest areas.

Nature is cyclical and compensatory.

Finally, the large number of anticulling proponents point out that the zoological formulas used to determine numbers to be culled from the population do not take the very substantial impact of poaching into full consideration.

There are some substitutes for elephant ivory to which the carvers might turn if they insist on continuing the industry. One natural substitute for elephant tusks is the store of ivory that the mammoths left behind in the permafrost of northern Asia when they faded into extinction. Russia has been harvesting limited amounts of these massive tusks for many years, and ivory-carving countries such as Japan have shown new interest in the product.

Other substitutes that have been considered are walrus tusks—which have been harvested for many years in the Soviet Union, Canada, and Alaska—and hippopotamus teeth. However, conservation agencies have expressed concern over the potential impact on both of these species. Turning to other animals for carving materials could easily result in the same crisis that developed with the elephant. Before elephant ivory was readily available in Europe, medieval carvers created so strong a market for walrus ivory that the once-vast herds of the North Sea were hunted to the brink of extinction.

THE ELEPHANT AND MAN

While the experts debate the issue, the elephants continue to crowd into the isolated pockets of even limited protection. Elephants have demonstrated a definite ability to recognize the differences between protected areas and areas where they are hunted. They show a natural inclination toward the former, which has served to increase the concentration of the huge animals into the wildlife reserves. In areas with significant poaching pressures, elephants may also switch to a largely nocturnal lifestyle. Particularly at concentrated spots, such as water holes, they may appear only under the cover of darkness, abandoning their natural habit of drinking and bathing several times during the day.

This is the second time around for the African elephant and severe population-wide decimation at the hands of man. From the earliest association of the two creatures, man has lusted for the magical whiteness of the elephant's ivory. Ornaments made of the lustrous material adorned the pharaohs and temples of Egypt.

The "white gold" business of ivory and the equally brutal but lucrative business of slavery coexisted for many generations of misery in Africa, long before the development of modern firearms. Long caravans of human beasts of burden, taken prisoner

oped for common consumption. Personal seals, which are the official signatures for much of the Japanese population, for example, are traditionally carved from ivory. Concerned wildlife officials, seeing what appeared to be the path to the total loss of all their elephant herds, began the move to more stringent control on hunting and the creation of national parks, where some measure of protection was afforded. Such action helped lead to an increase in the African elephant population from less than a million at the turn of the century to an estimated 1.5 million in 1970.

However the 114-dollar-per-pound high that ivory reached in Asian markets in 1989 was nine times the price paid in 1970. As a direct result, elephant numbers have dropped correspondingly: from 1.3 million in 1979, to 750,000 in 1987, and to 625,000 in 1989.

Ivory is riddled with tiny pores, filled with a waxlike gelatinous liquid. It is this fluid that gives a carved piece of ivory its lustrous, soft qualities. The ivory of the elephant cow generally offers a more desirable, finer grain than that of the bull. Further, ivory taken from a freshly murdered elephant— referred to as "live ivory"—is more desirable than that taken from long dead carcasses.

In addition, ivory taken from elephants of different regions tends to age differently. For example, that from Siamese elephants grows yellow, while that from West African animals grows whiter, and Ceylonese ivory becomes pinkish. The carving process begins with the removal of the outer shell of the tusk. The ivory that is exposed by this operation is then allowed to dry, taking on this darker quality as it does. Given the curved aspects of elephant tusks, most ivory carving has tended toward miniatures to allow for the eight-inch maximum length that can be obtained from even the largest tusk's straighter midsection.

A Long-Valued Commodity

Even before elephant ivory was being carved into the ornamentations of the first civilizations, primitive man was cutting crude representations from the ivory of mammoths. Examples of this work, dating to more than twenty thousand years ago, have been found throughout Europe, most notably in France.

in raids on villages across the continent, were forced to carry the ivory to the markets in the East, where both were sold. The seemingly endless expansion of one trade encouraged and fueled the prosperity of the other as well.

But the overall damage that man could wreak on elephant populations was greatly restricted until the mid-1800s, when modern, high-powered weaponry became commonly available. By the early 1900s, an estimated one hundred thousand elephants were being slaughtered each year to supply piano-key and billiard-ball manufacturers. The emergence of plastics in the 1940s, much cheaper and more readily available than ivory, greatly reduced demand for the elephant's elongated teeth.

Unfortunately, about this same time, ivory demand in the Far East was skyrocketing as new ornamental uses were being devel-

In Europe of the Middle Ages it was commonly believed that ivory came from the horn of the unicorn, which to people of that age was every bit as mythical or real as the strange elephants that they may or may not have heard about. At this time, only a few elephants had as yet been brought alive to Europe. One shown briefly in London in 1255 drew practically the entire populace of both the city and surrounding countryside for many miles. Perhaps the unicorn tale arose because some of the limited ivory that found its way to Europe during the period may have been the spiraled horns of narwhals, aquatic arctic mammals.

It is ironic that much ivory carving over the generations has depicted religious figures and scenes—such as the Madonna or the Crucifixion of Christ—when the raw material in reality reflects nothing but the most brutal of killing for the sake of profit. Just how many prayers have been issued in the presence of this symbol of elephant slaughter will never be known.

Elephants In Art, Literature, and Entertainment

The powerful, distinct lines of the elephant have captured the wonder and imagination of artists almost from the time the first primitive human put the symbol for some slaughtered animal on a cave wall. Prehistoric cave paintings depict elephants, along with great bisons, fierce boars, and the other strange creatures that filled early man's world. Some of these rocky depictions offer sad testimony to the much larger range once occupied by elephants, occurring as they do in caves many hundreds of miles from any present-day wild pachyderm.

Elephants are also the most commonly depicted animal in Indian and African art. Everything from clay to wood to ivory to brass has been fashioned into the image of the great beast. Finer work begins to appear around the third century B.C. in small ivory seals produced in India and in the fourth and fifth centuries B.C. in coins of the ancient city of Mathura (Muttra). Later, detailed paintings of elephants appeared on the walls of Egyptian tombs, such as that of Rameses III circa 1200 B.C.

Perhaps the animal's long association with religions in its home regions offers part of the explanation for its continued artistic popularity. The ancient Hindu religion, for example, portrayed the world in pyramidal terms. Elephants, due to their greatly respected strength, formed the base of that pyramid, supporting everything else on their broad backs.

The Hindu god Ganesh (who represents wisdom and success) sports the head of an elephant on a fat little body. The eight deities who guard the points of the Hindu compass are symbolized by elephants, which are also their assigned companion animals. A pair of elephants is believed to bring rain in that religion.

Additionally, the elephant has stood as a symbol of might from man's earliest encounters with the great beast. Tribal dances and tales throughout Africa, for example, often use the animal as the ultimate symbol of masculinity and power. Because the modern elephant developed in what man describes as the cradle of civilization—those areas thought to have first given rise to humans—it is one of the creatures that appears in the earliest writings of more civilized man as well.

Aristotle described the elephant in detail in his writings during the fourth century B.C. Kuo P'u, writing during the Chinese Chiu Dynasty in the third century B.C., described the largest land mammal as "a vast creature" with "the strength of ten bulls" and "a trunk which looks like a tail." Pliny the Elder wrote extensively about the pachyderm in his *Historia Naturalis* (*Natural History*) in A.D. 77. As a matter of fact, the elephant is first animal discussed in this landmark set of books. Much of what he wrote stands up to modern scrutiny. For example, he noted that elephants are "especially fond of water, and wander much about streams." However, he also spent much of the twelve chapters that he devoted to them in less accurate discourse. "These animals are well aware that the only spoil that we are anxious to procure of them is the part which forms their weapon of defense [the tusks]…when their tusks have fallen off, either by accident or from old age, they bury them in the earth….When they are surrounded by the hunters, they place those in front which have the smallest teeth, that the enemy may think that the spoil is not worth the combat."

Sadly, even at that early time, man had already had a noticeable impact on the species, because of those tusks that attracted so much of Pliny's attention. "Large teeth [meaning tusks] are now rarely found, except in India, the demands of luxury having exhausted all those in our part of the world," he wrote.

Similarly, from the earliest use of animals in entertainment, such as zoos and circuses, elephants seem to have been included in the menageries. As early as the ninth century B.C., members of Syrian royalty were displaying the animals in their private collections. The Romans, those enthusiastic patrons of all sorts of public events and exhibitions, had common viewings of the great pachyderms. The specimens were war elephants captured in battles with the Carthaginians in 251 B.C.

As often happened to new oddities in Roman society of the time, elephants soon showed up in the infamous "circuses." Around 130 B.C. they were added to the list of combatants—with gladia tors, bears, lions, tigers, rhinoceros, crocodiles, and so on—that did mortal battle in the arena. Other elephants were spared that brutality and, instead, were trained in a variety of performances.

Circuses of a different, more modern sort arose in Europe in the second half of the 1700s. Records of the first appearance by elephants in these events vary, although it certainly occurred prior to the first such appearance in an American circus in 1796. Jacob Crowninshield brought a two-year-old Asiatic female to New York City on April 13, 1796. It was the first elephant to come to America. The six-and-a-half-foot-tall pachyderm was exhibited at the corner of Broadway and Beaver Street. An amazed reporter for the New York *Argus* wrote that the animal "eats 30 pounds of rice besides, hay and straw. Drinks all kinds of wine and spirituous liquors, and eats every sort of vegetable. It will also draw a cork from a bottle with its trunk."

Most famous among all circus elephants was P.T. Barnum's Jumbo, which was probably also the largest bull elephant ever kept in captivity. The great showman claimed that his prize showpiece stood twelve feet tall at the shoulder. He never allowed exact measurements to be made, but independent evidence suggests that Jumbo was closer to eleven feet in height.

But it was Barnum's showmanship abilities that elevated the name of Jumbo to one that still sounds somehow familiar today. Jumbo began life like millions of other African elephants, in a herd in the region south of Lake Chad. The animal was captured during his juvenile years and placed in Paris' Jardin des Plantes, where it resided for a few years. The still-growing Jumbo was traded in 1865 to the Royal Zoological Gardens in London in exchange for a rhinoceros. Jumbo was put into service as a children's ride for several years, until the animal grew too uncontrollable for the task.

Barnum bought him for two thousand pounds in January 1882, a sale that led to a torrent of criticism—in letters from the public and in the newspapers—directed at the Royal Zoological Society and Barnum. Despite the misdirected outcry, Jumbo sailed for the United States on March 25, 1882. His career under Barnum's direction was short-lived, however, as the big elephant came to an untimely death on September 15, 1885, after being struck by a train in St. Thomas, Canada.

Barnum included a model of Jumbo, constructed from the elephant's hide, in his touring show for another two years. It was then moved into the Barnum Museum at Tufts University in Massachusetts, where it was consumed by fire in April 1975. Jumbo's skeleton was donated to the American Museum of Natural History in New York City.

Another elephant purchased for two thousand pounds brings us to the pachyderms of fiction and nursery rhymes. This particular elephant was Kiouni, the beast purchased by Phileas Fogg to carry his party along the Kholby-to-Allahabad leg of their trip *Around the World in Eighty Days* in the 1873 work by Jules Verne.

Far more famous of the elephants of literature is Babar, the baby separated from his mother and raised by humans as a child then adult of society. Others of this ilk include the Heffalump, the elephant of Piglet's dreams that he and Winnie the Pooh set out to capture; and the Elephant's Child from Rudyard Kipling's "Just So Stories," to name just a few.

Elephant Graveyard Myths

Modern knowledge tells us that the legendary "elephant graveyard" should be placed soundly into this same realm of fiction. However, this place where elephant after elephant comes to die has been sworn to by many native Africans and European explorers alike over the years. Huge piles of tusks have been cited as evidence of this site's existence, although there is usually some less-romantic explanation for the amassed ivory. There may be some basis to this legend, in that sick elephants very likely will seek out areas of convenient water and tender vegetation and more than one elephant may in time locate the same general vicinity as a final resting place. However, this is a far cry from the fabled valleys of ivory. Another explanation for these persistent tales might be that the observers have actually come onto the scene of a mass killing by poachers.

In addition, seventeenth-century ivory-traffickers were quick to grab hold of and promote the ancient African legends of the mass elephant graveyards. In those legends, they recognized a means of masking the fact that anyone with sufficient resources could buy all the tusks he wanted by traveling from one village to the next. And for some time their tales convinced much of the world that only they knew the hidden routes to the vast troves of ivory.

Elephants In War

Because of the elephant's huge size, mistakenly perceived ferocity, and weaponlike tusks, the animal has been as much a long-time, integral part of man's savagery as of his art and literature. Perhaps the most commonly known use of the elephant as an instrument of war was the 219 B.C. crossing of the Alps by Hannibal.

The Carthaginian general actually had only three dozen elephants in his forces, and certainly lost at least some of these in the crossing. But the fact that he and his men could get even some of the huge tropical beasts over the snow-covered mountains and into Rome carved the image of that crossing into mankind's common memory.

In addition, the elephants proved powerful weapons in subsequent battles, such as that at Trebia. Early historians tell us that soldiers in the Roman armies were unable to stand up against the approaching animals, while horses—catching their first glimpses and scents of the odd creatures—reared out of control and fled in terror.

After his victory at Trebia, Hannibal made another mountainous crossing with his elephants. But this time the unaccustomed environment and the rigors of the march took a heavier toll. According to some accounts, when Hannibal finally set foot on the far side of the Apennines, only the general's own pachyderm survived.

Although elephants do not appear to have been used for direct warfare by most Chinese armies, Marco Polo brought back one account of such use from his travels in the East. Of the attack by

Kublai Khan on his rebellious cousin Nayan, sometime between 1275 and 1294, he wrote as follows:

Kublai took his station in a large wooden castle, borne on the backs of four elephants, whose bodies were protected with coverings of thick leather hardened by fire, over which were housings of cloth of gold. The castle contained many crossbow men and archers, and on top of it was hoisted the imperial standard.

However, the European adventurer's account of his travels do relate the regular use of elephants by armies opposing the Khan conquests. According to Marco Polo, on learning of the approach of several of the Khan's armies, the king of Mien and Bangala "assembled a very large army, including a multitude of elephants (an animal with which his country abounds) upon whose backs were placed battlements or castles, of wood, capable of containing to the number of twelve or sixteen men in each."

The elephants proved crucial in the early battles, until the Khan's commander on the scene adapted a strategy of falling back into a heavily wooded area and having his archers pellet the elephants with their arrows. Pincushioned with arrows, the terrified animals were no longer controllable by their drivers and began to crash in retreat into and over the king's armies.

Even Alexander the Great ran up against the obstacle that elephants could present in 326 B.C., when he led his armies against Punjab (northern India). He expected only light opposition, but at the Jhelum River, King Porus met the advance with a force of thirty-four thousand men and more than two hundred war elephants. The invaders' horses were terrified of the elephants and were generally impossible to control in the battle. As a result, Alexander's invasion was extended many more weeks than he had originally planned. It was nonetheless successful.

Because of the prevalence of war elephants throughout regions they had targeted for conquest, military leaders of the Roman Empire designed elaborate defenses against the animals. Soldiers equipped with javelins and arrows were positioned to attack the approaching elephants. Their barrage of sharp objects killed very few of the pachyderms but often proved successful in irritating the animals to the point that their handlers could no longer manage them. When fire was added to their projectiles, the effect on the ele-

phants was even more dramatic. The terror-filled animals often turned on their own armies, which in turn had to destroy them or be destroyed. Other soldiers, armed with axes, attacked the legs of the elephants, in attempts to hamstring and cripple them or mortally injure their belly areas. Elephants captured in battle were regularly employed in the Roman attempts to perfect these techniques. Others were destroyed in the arena to debunk popular myths about their supreme power and invincibility.

Despite their development of these successful antielephant techniques, the Romans sometimes employed the animals in their own armies. Several phalanxes of sixty-four elephants—complete with their human riders, saddlers, and cooks (one each per elephant)— were organized and deployed. Accounts of conquests against the Carthaginians and the Gauls reflect successful Roman use of the animals.

Elephants At Work

African elephants certainly can be trained to perform tasks for man, but the Asiatic elephant has a much longer working tradition. Asiatic elephants taken from the wild can be tamed very quickly. African elephants, even when captured as very young infants, are much slower to accept their new situation.

Records indicate that the Asiatic animals were doing heavy labor in logging operations in the mountainous regions of Asia as early as 2000 B.C. Some are still used in this manner, while others are now hauling loads of tourists into national parks.

The earliest existing records of tamed elephants—known as

kunki in India—are found on ornamental seals from India that date from 1500 B.C. The association of man and elephant in some sort of working relationship, however, probably extends even further back into history. These seals clearly depict the use of a howdah on the elephant's back, a seating device still used today that must have been developed over an extended period of man's use of the animals. Until recent years, the new stock of work elephants was always collected from the wild in drives that captured entire herds at a time. Elephant drives to collect wild stock, known as *khedda* in India, traditionally involve hundreds or even thousands of drivers and dozens of domestic elephants. Progressing over several weeks, the drivers and domestic elephants gradually encircle the area inhabited by a wild herd and then slowly close that circle in the direction of a large enclosed spot. The drive is tightly choreographed so that all parts of the circle converge on the enclosure at the same time. Only the sturdiest young females are selected for training, and the rest are allowed to return to the jungle.

Although India recently placed a ban on the removal of elephants from the wild for domestication, the wild remains the primary source for new stock. Mahouts (elephant keepers and drivers) are reluctant to let one of their workers take several years off for pregnancy and rearing of a baby. Despite the preference of their handlers, work elephants do breed quite readily. The offspring in the past have been sold as quickly as possible to animal dealers, to allow the females to get back to work.

In addition to training at the hands of humans, which is well under way by the time the animal is three years old, elephants are quick to pick up the habits, manners, and tricks of the older members of the working group into which they are placed. Training is generally conducted by the same mahout, who will work with the elephant throughout its useful life. The first step is to break the wild beast's spirit, similar to what the American cowboy did with wild horses in the West. The wild elephant is tied out without food until it reaches the state of semistarvation and weakness; at this point, it begins to obey the mahout's commands to obtain even the most meager morsel of food.

After several years of training in increasingly strenuous and rigorous tasks, the elephant is ready for hard labor in the logging camps. By then, it has mastered about three dozen different commands and displays a special affection for the mahout, whom it has come to see as its sole source of food and water.

In addition to using verbal commands, a mahout controls an elephant with a great deal of body language. The trainer sits astride the elephant's neck, with legs and feet positioned just behind the animal's ears. If the mahout stiffens his legs and leans backwards, the elephant knows to stop. Pressure exerted with either leg tells the elephant the direction in which to move. By leaning forward and pressing down with the body, the mahout conveys his charge to kneel. For emphasis or punishment, the mahout sometimes jabs the elephant with his ankus, a sharp instrument that delivers an unpleasant prick to the animal.

Working elephants in India are able to haul weights of up to two tons each by dragging the load behind them. On their backs, however, they can carry less than a half ton. Some mahouts allow their elephants occasional free time, albeit under hobbled conditions, to wander through the jungle near the camp, browsing on the vegetation.

Of course, not all trained elephants spend their lives in the hard drudgery of logging camp operations. A few today, and quite a few more in past periods, are reserved for ceremonial purposes. According to accounts of a 1795 wedding of a ranking official of India, nearly twelve hundred "richly caparisoned" elephants were involved in the procession. A full one hundred of them were adorned with howdahs made of silver or gold and inlaid with gems.

In addition, many elephants are pressed into service in the region's growing tourist industry to provide visitors with "authentic" elephant-back safaris. In this case, a very thick blanket is strapped to the elephant's back, much as a blanket is placed under a saddle on a horse's back, and a howdah is also part of the equipment.

The diet of a working elephant generally consists of plenty of leafy tree branches of various species, sugarcane, wheat cakes, boiled rice, sugar, salt, and occasional treats of fruits. The government and the lumber companies tend to monitor closely the conditions under which the animals are maintained, particularly in relation to their food.

Elephants As Aggressors

As would be expected, over the generations of such close association with the animals, several thousand people have lost their lives to elephants, although this is less than a drop in the bucket when compared to the many millions of elephants that man has destroyed. Reports of such incidents have been emerging from the wilds of Africa and southeast Asia for centuries.

One of the most recent reports came from the tiny Indonesian village of Panggung in July 1990, after a herd of Asiatic elephants "attacked," killed one man, destroyed the villagers' crops, and chased the people from their homes. The *Jakarta Post* quoted the village chief as attributing the attack to the elephants taking revenge because of elephant carcasses left near the village by ivory poachers.

African elephants occasionally wreak similar havoc among small villages. But more often the elephants—of either species— simply wander into villages and cause some damage without injuring anyone. Sometimes their actions have a deliberate flair about them, while at other times they can only be described as accidental. Regardless, the results are generally damaged dwellings and crops, but there are rarely deaths or injuries among the humans.

For some reason, African elephants also from time to time declare war on some of man's smaller constructions within their territories. Signs are a particular target, being uprooted and removed repeatedly or even buried under small stacks of sticks. Telephone poles have also been pulled from their base and laid on the ground.

A new phenomenon, particularly in some of Africa's parks with denser elephant populations, is a type of elephant that has been nicknamed the "tourist elephant." Like bears in some of America's national parks, these elephants have come to associate humans and their vehicles with food because of handouts from previous tourists. They have been known to damage cars and threaten the occupants to get at the "goodies."

In another habit shared with America's park bears, some of these same tourist elephants have also taken to scavenging in garbage cans. Once they've become accustomed to this behavior, the elephants tend to lose any discrimination in what they eat from the cans and can ingest items such as plastic bags, which are injurious to their systems.

In very rare instances an elephant does go through with the full charge and attack, generally with results that can indeed be shocking. Dismemberment with that powerful trunk is a common thread running through many of these reports. Impalement on the tusks is another. And, of course, when an elephant has a mind to do it, just a few steps of the animal are enough to completely crush a human.

But, again, it cannot be overly emphasized that these attacks are very much out of the ordinary and often exaggerated in the retelling. Such embellishment can be seen in G.P. Sanderson's *Thirteen Years Among the Wild Beasts of India*. He recounts:

> Of cases recorded of really vicious animals perhaps the most notable is that of the Mandla [near Jubbulpore, Central Provinces] elephants, an elephant supposed to have been made, and which killed an immense number of persons about five years ago. It is said to have eaten portions of some of its victims, but it probably only held their limbs in its mouth whilst it tore them to pieces.

Most human injuries and deaths, however, are not without some reason on the elephant's part. Tourists who disregard park warnings and signs about getting out of their vehicles, feeding the animals, and the like are prime targets. Poachers are also justifiably at risk.

As familiar as the elephant may seem on first mention, it is actually a very mysterious animal that we are only beginning to understand. It's generally a gentle creature capable of actions involving great strength and power. It's an incredibly emotional and caring animal; many would say, as emotional and caring as our own species.

Above everything else, however, the elephant is an animal dangerously close to the edge of extinction. We could very well push the earth's entire remaining population over that edge if we're not very thoughtful and careful in this last decade of the twentieth century.

For many, the passing of the elephant as a species, or two species, would be nothing more than one more footnote to the book of devastation that mankind has written for so many of the fellow travelers on this planet.

But, for many others, for a growing number of citizens of the earth, the loss of the elephant would be a tragedy of unmatched proportions. The question is often heard: If the elephant can't be saved, can man?

Feasting with gusto on the lush vegetation of Aberdare National Park, Kenya, a bull elephant is nonetheless alert to the presence of the photographer.

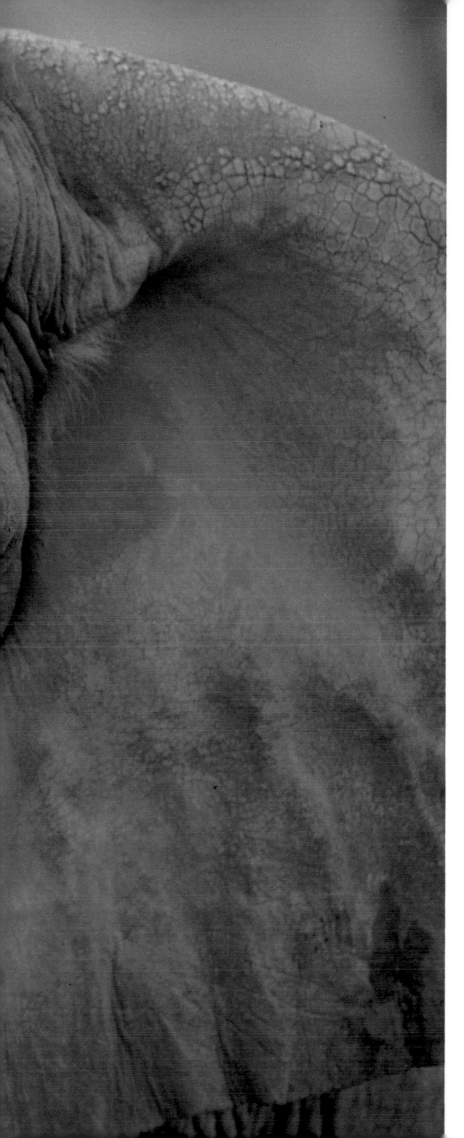

THE LARGEST LIVING LAND MAMMAL

Almost every schoolchild can tell you: The elephant is the largest living land animal. Few other creatures come close, in size or in sheer bulk. However, the elephant is the not largest animal on earth. That honor is held by the blue whale, which can reach lengths of 100 feet and weigh nearly 125 tons. The elephant must also give way in the category of tallest land animal, a title held by the giraffe, with its potential stretch of nineteen feet.

Of the two species of elephant alive today, the African elephant is by far the larger. The largest African bull on record stood twelve feet, six inches at the shoulder. From tip of extended trunk to tip of extended tail, its measurement was thirty-three feet, two inches. Its body girth was recorded as nineteen feet, eight inches. Referred to as the Fenykoevi elephant—in deference to the Hungarian big-game hunter that shot it on November 13, 1955, near Macusso, Angola—this bull has been on display in the entrance hall of the United States National Museum of Natural History in Washington, D.C., since March 6, 1959.

While the Fenykoevi elephant was estimated to have weighed more than 74,000 pounds, which seems reasonable for that size elephant, the greatest accurately recorded weight of any elephant is 14,641 pounds. This was the weight of a large bull killed on December 26, 1935, near Ngaruka, Tanzania. The body was cut into 176 individual segments that were then weighed individually on scales with capacities of 600 pounds. The loss of blood and other body liquids during this laborious process certainly reduced the weight that was finally recorded.

The largest Asiatic elephant ever recorded measured eleven feet, nine inches at the highest point on its arching back and eleven feet, one inch at the shoulder. Both measurements would have been a few inches less had the animal been standing rather than lying on its side. Its weight was estimated to be sixteen thousand pounds. W.H. Varian shot this elephant in Sri Lanka in 1882.

The greatest weight ever accurately recorded for an Asiatic elephant

The elephant's brain is relatively large, measuring about a foot in diameter, compared to that of many other animals. However, in relation to body size, the brain is only about one-tenth as large as that of humans. Nevertheless, the elephant is one of the most intelligent creatures.

The African bush at sunset is a mysterious place, filled with unexpected sounds and sights, such as the sudden emergence of a passing elephant.

was 14,313 pounds. This was the bull Tusko, whose life ended on June 10, 1934, in the Woodland Park Zoological Garden in Seattle, Washington.

Size and Body Temperature

Such incredible size has several advantages. The elephant has few natural enemies. Man is its greatest threat by far, and other than his predations, only the very young elephants are vulnerable to some of the big cats, such as leopards. The elephant can move relatively large distances over short periods of time. It is a long-lived creature, at least those individuals that escape the poachers. Additionally, the animal's imposing head allows for a large brain capacity and intelligence that we are only beginning to understand.

Of course, with all those advantages come a few notable drawbacks.

Elephants never stop growing throughout their lifetime and, thus, size is a reliable indicator of age: The larger the elephant, the older it is.

Great volumes of food and water are required every day to power such a large frame. An elephant's digestive system makes full use of only forty percent of the nutrients that the animal consumes. To compensate for this low internal efficiency, the elephant spend nearly two-thirds of every day eating approximately three hundred to five hundred pounds of vegetation.

Body-temperature regulation is another disadvantage faced by such large animals. All mammals, from the smallest pygmy shrew to the towering elephant, need to maintain internal temperatures within a range of only a few degrees throughout the year and throughout their lives. For example, the average temperature for man is 98.6 degrees Fahrenheit, while the average for the elephant—which might weight seventy-five times as much as a man —is 97.1 degrees Fahrenheit.

Mammalian bodies produce heat by burning food to provide energy for all functions of the body. Therefore, the larger the body, the more heat that is produced. Heat is lost from the body through the skin, which

Despite their bulk, elephants are able to move through thick bush country with surprisingly little commotion. The soft soles of this big animal's feet are spongy and are therefore able to absorb quite a bit of noise.

Despite its massive bulk, the elephant can reach speeds of twenty-five miles per hour over short distances. Observers have noted more than one type of running behavior in the animals, including the fast, direct panic run and the trumpeting, ear- and trunk-flailing joyful run.

larger mammals have less of in proportion to their overall body size.

Given these conditions, it becomes obvious that the elephant has a relatively large bodily capacity for generating heat, but a relatively small bodily capacity for losing that heat. Keeping cool is an almost constant obsession with elephants. It is one function of the massive ears to provide additional skin surface to radiate that heat out of the body.

Movement

Despite the elephant's great bulk, the animal has the ability to move almost silently through even dense brush. The incredible weight of each step is absorbed by a cushionlike layer of tissue that covers the base of each foot.

In their normal, undisturbed movements, a herd of elephants will amble about at just four miles per hour. However, when startled or threatened, the same animals will crash through the brush or charge an enemy at more than twenty-five miles per hour.

The steep banks along this Kenyan river pose little obstruction to an elephant family.

The shape of the elephant is one of the most instantly recognizable ones of the natural world. School children across the globe can make a correct identification, even if they've never seen a live specimen.

An elephant's eye is very small in relation to the rest of its head and contains relatively few photoreceptors. Consequently, the animal does not see well beyond several hundred feet.

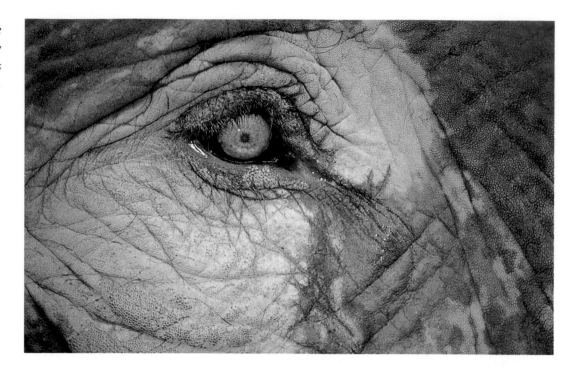

A herd of springbok, a South African gazelle, parts to allow a trio of African elephant bulls access to a water hole. Despite this instance, the huge tuskers often fail to capitalize on their incredible size advantage.

Although elephants can reach such speeds over short distances, they cannot gallop like horses. Elephants do not run or trot or move in any manner other than a walk. They can walk very fast, in a shuffling fashion, considerably faster than a man can run. But they can do no more. They also cannot jump. Walls, even those of medium height, are enough of an obstacle to cause the animals to change their route.

The elephant is also a much better swimmer than its size and build reveal. Although it generally prefers wading through the shallows, it is rarely hesitant to take to lakes or rivers and then to swim for considerable distances when such action serves its purpose. In deep water, the elephant keeps its trunk out of the water, in periscope fashion.

Climbing steep, hilly, and mountainous areas is another ability that might not casually be attributed to any creature with the bulk of an elephant, but the species is generally skilled—if slow and methodical—at the task. They have a marvelous sense of balance and are as sure-footed as any creature. They also tend to test out any uncertain spots with their trunks before placing their feet on them.

An Indian elephant hoists itself from the river after a refreshing bath. The cooling effect of the waters is essential to lowering the elephant's body temperature. It also helps to remove insects and other pests.

A young tusker tries to grasp individual fruits dangling overhead with its trunk. A larger elephant might simply wrap its muscular trunk about the tree base and shake the fruits to the ground, where they could be collected by the agile "fingers" at the trunk's tip and deposited into its mouth.

Physical Characteristics

Although the tale of the six blind men who went to study an elephant was written as a moralistic Hindu scripture, its telling also reveals just what an odd collection of parts this big animal is. The first man felt the animal's large, sturdy side and de scribed it as similar to a wall. The second felt the tusk and pronounced the elephant similar to a spear. The third felt the trunk and described the animal as snakelike. The fourth encountered the knee and thought the elephant was like the tree. The fifth touched the ear and said the beast was like a fan. Finally, the sixth felt the tail and described the elephant as being similar to a rope.

The moral, by the way, is this: Although none of the six had actually seen the elephant and each was basing his description on only a small, selective perception, each one was prepared to vigorously

A young elephant fills its mouth with water at the edge of the Savuti Channel in Chobe National Park, Botswana.

Laden with grass, an Indian elephant heads back to camp in Manas Tiger Reserve, India. Although the mahouts put their beasts of burden through strenuous paces, the animals are well fed and cared for.

Elephants have adapted to the encroachment of human beings on their ancestral ranges. Here, African elephants are shown drinking from a water tank. This familiarity can lead to conflict, and the elephants are usually the losers.

dispute the convictions of his fellows. Another lesson, more appropriate to our discussion, might be: Exactly which of the elephant's strange features is the most unique?

With the tip of its trunk pointed into the wind, an African bull tests the breeze for scents.

The Trunk

The trunk, which is unique to the proboscidian family, probably is the most notable aspect among other unusual features of the elephant. Sometime around 50 to 45 B.C., a Roman poet named Lucre tius described the elephant as "the beast that hath between his eyes, a serpent for a hand." This magnificent appendage is actually a boneless, muscular elongation of the upper lip and nose. It measures almost three feet around at the base and is composed of an estimated forty thousand muscles.

It is among the most versatile of all mammalian creations. Powerful enough to kill a lion with a single blow, the fingerlike lobes at the tip of the trunk are still adept enough to pluck a feather from the ground. Nearly all of the fifty gallons of water that an adult elephant drinks every day is drawn

Due to their huge body size and the incredible reach of their trunks, elephants are able to forage from branches that are quite high off the ground. In some areas of Africa, a "browse line" is evident at about twenty feet.

The trunk of the elephant—which functions as a nose, arm, hand, and multipurpose tool —is equipped with more than forty thousand muscles. It is powerful enough to deliver a crushing blow and yet dexterous enough to pick up a feather.

Stripping the bark from this tree may prove too much of a task for this young African elephant. More often, the babies must content themselves with scavenging scraps left by their elders.

through the nostrils at the tip of the trunk—up to a gallon and a half on each draft—and squirted into the mouth. Similarly, the five hundred pounds of vegetation that make up the menu for one elephant are plucked, pulled, and ripped with the trunk and placed into the mouth.

The same appendage is used to scoop up and hurl dust over the animal several times a day. Some of the elephant's vocalizations, including the famous trumpeting call, are sounded through the trunk. The same nostril openings are the connection to the world for the elephant's powerful sense of smell, which can pick scent off the wind at more than two miles distant.

The elephant is instinctively aware of the importance of the trunk to its life and lifestyle. A severe enough injury to that marvelous proboscis could result in the animal's death. Some, however, have been known to survive many years even with severe damage that made their trunks virtually useless. They show a remarkable range of adaptations to their new situations, such as kneeling to eat grass or to drink water directly with their mouths. They are nevertheless hindered from many essential elephant activities. When danger is detected, the elephant coils its trunk tightly and holds it close to the body. They tend to rest the great weight of their trunks in surprising manners while they sleep, such as coiling them like a snake and resting them on a tusk.

Many individuals have also developed the trunk skill of tossing food items into their mouths from several inches away and thus saving themselves valuable time and effort that can be employed to gather even more food when at a particularly plentiful source. Elephants are born with some abilities to use their trunks, such as exchanging tender touches with their mothers. In a handlike use, baby elephants often insert their trunks into their mouths and suck on them, like a human child sucks on its thumb. But most of the myriad uses must be learned and mastered over the first few years of life. For example, the youngster accompanies its family group to a water hole, but must bend its entire body to get its mouth to the quenching water. Eventually, on of these frequent excursions, it will chance to place a wet trunk into its mouth and the learning process has begun.

At the tip of the trunk there is a fingerlike structure that the elephant can manipulate much like we humans move our fingers. The Asiatic elephant has one such protrusion at the upper side, while

A juvenile African elephant strips bark from a tree, using its tusks to gouge and cut into the bark and its trunk to grasp and rip. The laborious process is generally confined to those times when other food sources are scarce.

Elephants show a decided preference for drinking water with high mineral concentrations and will travel great distances to find suitable water holes.

When browsing on branches far overhead, the elephant wraps its trunk around the foliage and tugs downward.

the African elephant has both upper and lower "fingers."

Among the many fictional explanations—and there are many—for the elephant's extraordinary trunk, the most widely known is probably that offered by Rudyard Kipling in "The Elephant's Child," one of the author's "Just So Stories."

"In the high and Far-Off Times the Elephant, O Best Beloved, had no trunk. He had only a blackish, bulgy nose, as big as a boot, that he could wriggle from side to side; but he couldn't pick things up with it," Kipling began his tale. Into this situation enters a new elephant, the Elephant's Child, "who was full of 'satiable curtiosity."

This "curtiosity" leads him to the banks of a great river in search of the answer to his latest question: "What does the Crocodile have for dinner?" He finally poses his question to the croc, who tricks him into venturing too close and grabs the short, stubby nose of the Elephant's Child in his mouth. In response the young elephant "sat back on his little haunches, and pulled, and pulled, and pulled, and his nose began to stretch. And the Croco dile floundered into the water, making it all

Elephant tusks are elongated upper-incisor teeth. They grow continuously throughout the elephant's life. The two sides of a pair have often been found to vary a few inches from an exact match, depending on whether the animal favors its right or left side.

Close inspection reveals the incredible strength of the elephant's trunk—power enough to kill a full-grown cow with a single swing.

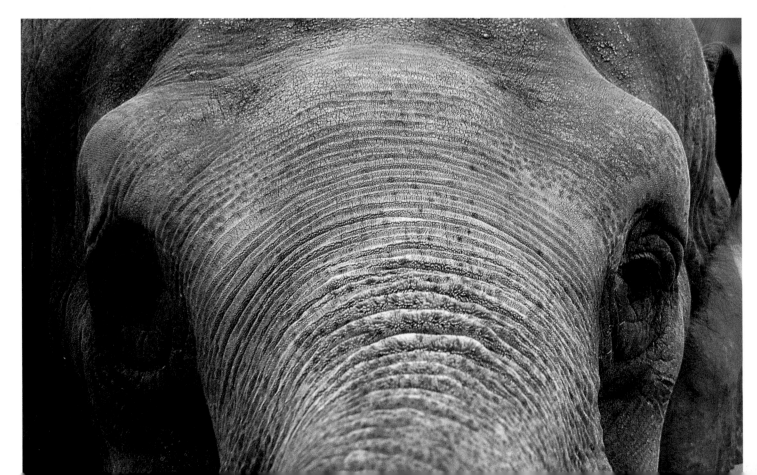

creamy with great sweeps of his tail, and he pulled, and pulled, and pulled.

"And the Elephant's Child's nose kept on stretching; and the Elephant's Child spread all his little four legs and pulled, and pulled, and pulled, and his nose kept on stretching; and the Crocodile threshed his tail like an oar, and he pulled, and pulled, and pulled, and at each pull the Elephant's Child's nose grew longer and longer."

With the eventual aid of a "Bi-Coloured-Python-Rock-Snake," the Elephant's Child was able to wrench his now greatly elongated proboscis from the crocodile's grasp. At first the young elephant tries to shrink his trunk back to its original nose size. But with the further help of the snake, he comes to realize the many benefits of such a unique instrument, including spanking all his family and friends back home—the same creatures who had repeatedly spanked him for all his questions.

Enjoying a bath in the river, a baby Indian elephant sprays a drink from its trunk into its mouth.

The Tusks

A second distinctive feature of the elephant is also the cause of the animal's arrival at the brink of extinction. Those tusks of ivory have been prized by generations of man for the beautiful sculptures and ornamentation that can be carved from them.

Actually, the tusks are enlarged and protruding incisor teeth that have been recorded at more than 10.5 feet in the largest African bulls. Each tusk holds a cone-shaped cavity that extends from the jawbone to about the first third or the middle of the tusk's length and contains nerve tissue. The rest of the tusk is completely solid from that point forward. As much as one-third of each tusk is contained in the animal's upper jawbone.

These tusks receive rough treatment through their daily use and consequently are worn down a bit every day. Additionally, elephants show a right-handed or left-handed tendency in the use of their tusks, making much more use of one over the other. This tendency will generally be reflected in the relative sizes of the two tusks, with the preferred side showing much more wear than the other. However, the tusks continue to grow throughout the animal's life. Theoretically, the tusks of a bull could reach phenomenal proportions by the end of a full, sixty-year life. But lifespans of that duration are virtually unheard of today, and tusks are generally broken off much shorter than their full potential.

As tusks are actually elongated incisor teeth, they are covered with the normal tooth surface of enamel. Ivory is actually a blend of this enamel, the dentine material beneath, cartilage, and mineral deposits.

Rather than bending over to place their mouths in the water, as most other animals do, elephants use their trunks to draw large volumes of water into their mouths.

The Teeth

The elephant's mouth is also equipped with four molars—one on each side of both the upper and lower jaws—which are used in grinding its food. In an adult elephant, each one of these molars measures about four inches in width by a foot in length. Over the years, these molars wear down and are replaced by others that move forward in the mouth. At about forty years of age, the last available set moves into place.

Each half of each jaw will hold a half-dozen molars over the life of the elephant, but no more than two at the same time. The first and second molars are available in newborn calves. As the animal

40

Water fills the air as an African elephant tries to wet its entire body using a small, shallow water hole. The cooling effect of the water is essential to the animal's well-being, and in extreme drought conditions elephants have been known to extract water from their own throats to wet their ears.

A lone African elephant moves through grasslands in the shadow of Mount Kilimanjaro in Amboseli National Park, Kenya.

chews the rough material that makes up much of the elephant's diet, the molars gradually break away in layers. The first molars are completely worn away by the age of three to five. The second lasts for another half-dozen years. Sometime between the loss of the first and second molars, the third one comes into play. The fourth can appear any time between age six and thirty and the fifth anytime between sixteen and forty-five.

Each subsequent molar is larger than the last, and by the time the sixth one comes in—sometime in the animal's early thirties— they have reached the size of bricks. Each new molar also carries more ridges,

Elephants spray spouts of water from their trunks both to refresh themselves, as this Indian bull elephant demonstrates, and to express irritation. The most famous instance of the latter occurred in 1514, when an elephant that had been forced by its handler to bow for the Pope drew a trunkful of water from a trough and sprayed the entire assemblage, including His Holiness.

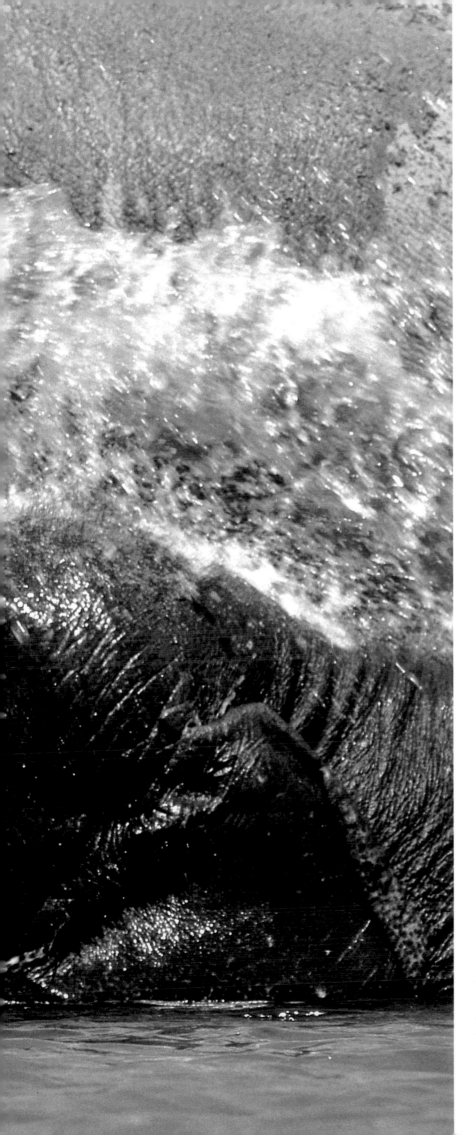

What youngster would not revel in the built-in squirt gun with which the baby elephant is naturally provided? However, elephants rarely use their trunks to spray one another.

Elephants generally take advantage of the relatively cool temperatures of early morning to move from their feeding areas of the night to refreshing water holes for the day.

The heaviest pair of tusks ever recorded belonged to a bull African elephant. They weighed just over 440 pounds. Growth rate varies among elephants but continues throughout the animal's life. In males, the rate even accelerates with age.

which are important in grinding the elephant's food, than its predecessor. The exact number of ridges ranges from four in the first molar to twenty-four in the sixth.

Life is tough on these grinding teeth and, in the very rare event that an elephant attains the full lifespan of sixty-plus years, it will likely has lost all of its teeth. None can be replaced at this time of life, and the dental problem may very likely result in the animal's death from starvation. This situation is one reason that the elephant's full life expectancy is a bit less than that of humans.

The Ears

While pachyderm hearing is more acute than was once believed, the huge ears serve a much more important function in helping to cool the animal. They are packed with blood vessels and when flapped—an

Researchers who spend a great deal of time observing elephants have devised a number of systems for identifying individual animals. One method involves the ears, in which the vein patterns are as distinctive as human fingerprints.

Elephant skin is much more sensitive than it appears on first inspection. Sun, heat, insects, and injuries all take their toll. The elephant counterattacks with mud, dirt, and sand, showering its entire body or rolling in these substances regularly.

action that increases substantially with even a half-degree rise in air temperature—quickly lower the animal's body temperature via its swiftly circulating blood.

The circulatory system of the elephant carries an enormous capacity to move blood through the animal's body. The heart of an adult elephant weighs more than twenty-five pounds, and arteries have diameters that range to more than three-quarters of an inch. By comparison the average human heart weighs about ten ounces, and only the aorta nears three-quarters of an inch. This is important in many of the elephant's reactions to its environment, such as a much higher tolerance for cold than for heat. Working elephants, for example, must be rested from midmorning to midafternoon each day.

Swifter ear flapping is also an aggressive action, although it is not generally associated with actual charges. When an elephant senses something out of the ordinary within close proximity, one of the

The trunk is an incredible tool, used in virtually all elephant activities and rituals. It is equipped with thousands of muscles.

"When people call this beast to mind, they marvel more and more; at such a little tail behind, so a large a trunk before," wrote English author Hilaire Belloc of the elephant.

Covered from head to toe with thick mud, a cow and her calf emerge from a mud bath. While the mud acts as a cooling agent for the elephants, its primary purpose is to provide a sticky base to hold the cleansing dust that they will soon blow onto themselves.

indications of its agitated curiosity is rapid ear flapping. Probably for this reason, the action is never as pronounced among less dominant animals within a grouping, at least not when the more dominant animals are close at hand.

All this special apparatus carries a great deal of weight that the elephant's neck must support, but this is somewhat compensated for by the several spongelike areas in the massive head. Without this weight reduction, mature elephants with fully developed tusks would have great difficulty moving and making much use at all of these important tools. These spongy areas are lined with mucous membranes, similar to those located in the nose.

Skin, Hair, and Grooming

Over all these muscles and organs stretches a skin that is three-quarters to an inch-and-a-half thick, generally reaching its greatest thickness at the hind end of the animal. Folds commonly form in the skin at various locations on the body, but particularly toward the hind end. Many different species of insects inhabit these folds, causing much discomfort for the elephant.

Baby elephants generally begin life with a gray-black skin that gradually takes on a pink-white tint. This tinting process most often begins at the trunk, ears, eyes, and neck. A few babies begin life with the pink-white color, and these are particularly esteemed in east Asia.

As tough as the thick hide of the elephant may appear to us, it is actually quite susceptible to the ravages of insects and heat. Because of this, a rigorous ritual of skin care is generally followed on a daily basis. First, the elephant luxuriates in an oozing mud hole, rolling head to toe in the wonderful muck. This is followed by a heavy dusting of dry earth, which the elephant hurls over itself with its trunk. Much color variation that has been noted in elephants by newcomer observers can be attributed to the color of the soil they've been using for their dust bathing. Finally, all those hard-to-reach spots, such as the rump, as rubbed against the nearest coarse surface. The huge, cementlike termite hills that are common features of the African landscape are particularly favored for this final task.

A weather-beaten tree affords a handy scratching post to reach a difficult, itchy spot on this Indian elephant's trunk. Elephants engage in a great deal of scratching against conveniently located objects in their constant struggle to rid themselves of insects and parasites.

With a gentle nudge, the next bather takes its place at the mud hole. Mud baths are as important to the elephant's continued existence as food and water, providing the starting point for the extensive daily grooming ritual.

Among the many insects and parasites that plague the elephant, the tick is among the most bothersome. The huge pachyderms can grasp the bloodsuckers' bodies with the tips of their trunks, but are generally unable to remove them in this way. The engorged ticks most often fall off after taking on all the blood that their bodies can hold or are crushed during the elephants' scratching against hard objects.

Except for a subspecies of the Asiatic elephant, pachyderms normally enter life with much more hair than they will carry into adulthood. Newborns emerge with bodywide coverings of thin, brownish hair. Scattered hairs can be found at any spot on the adult's body, but mostly at the eyes and forehead, as well as on the tail.

Elephants are equally painstaking in their care of certain internal areas. They regularly reach inside

An African bull digs more dirt with its trunk to get its mud bath just right. Although they have not been classified among the few animals that make and use tools, elephants exhibit remarkable ingenuity in adapting their environment to suit their needs.

A bull Indian elephant pauses to scratch an itch. Although the skin appears quite tough, the elephant is plagued by many parasites.

A young bull tries to intimidate an observer in Tsavo National Park, Kenya. Actual full charges that end in physical contact are extremely rare—not only between elephants but also between elephants and other creatures, such as humans.

Nearly every elephant engages in a greeting ceremony upon meeting one or more of its own kind. The intensity of the greeting varies with how close the two elephants or two groups have been in the past.

The huge ears of the elephant provide an impressive cooling system for the animal. Blood leaving the ear has been gauged at fifteen degrees Fahrenheit cooler than blood entering that same ear.

their ear cavities with the tips of their trunks or twigs held in their trunks and twist about to clean out the area. They also clean their noses by placing their trunks—one nostril at a time—over their tusk or some other handy object and twisting it.

The Feet

African elephants generally have five toes on each foot, while the average Asiatic elephant have five toes on each forefoot and four on each hindfoot. Mahouts (elephant handlers) especially prize Asiatic elephants with five toes on all four feet and are willing to pay extra to obtain them. The outer toe on each foot is usually nothing more than a rudiment of the other toes and generally lacks a toenail.

The skin on the sole of each foot is much softer than would be expected but contains many hardened areas. Elephants surprisingly do much of their walking on the tips of their toes. The area of the leg that we might assume to be the elephant's knee actually functions like our wrist. The sole of the foot acts as a cushion, expanding under the weight of each step, thus alleviating some of the strain on the leg.

However, the leg is well designed for carrying a heavy load. The bones are extraordinarily thick and without any soft marrow areas. For many years it was generally assumed that another reason for the massive, well-balanced legs was because adult elephants never laid down to sleep. However, this has been disproved and is further discussed in the last chapter of this book.

Dust fills the air as elephants at the Samburu National Reserve, Kenya, shower themselves with dry earth. After this grooming process is concluded, the elephants will seek rough objects in the immediate vicinity to rub against. Sun-baked termite hills are favorite rubbing stations.

Elephants sometimes appear to be different colors on account of the dust and mud with which they have covered themselves. Some elephants, like this Indian one, even look near-pink for this reason.

The plains and hills of Tarangire National Park in Tanzania are the breathtaking habitat for this African elephant.

A herd does some last-minute dusting before moving off to its nocturnal feeding grounds in Mana Pools National Park, Zimbabwe.

ENVIRONMENTAL IMPACT

The effects of elephants on their environment is another area of knowledge that is only beginning to develop. It has been obvious for some time that these enormous creatures can quickly and efficiently change a given area in their search for food. However, the relationship of this to overall changes in habitat and the impact of those changes on other wildlife is now being studied.

As it has for millions of years, elephant activity in the jungle regions opens areas of the rainforest and permits new ground-level growth to occur. Such vegetation is important to ground-foraging creatures. Without the elephantine impacts, the upper story of the rainforest might prevent ground growth for many additional generations.

The impact that the elephants' ravenous appetites can have on other species was brought home clearly in the early 1960s in Tsavo National Park in Kenya. The concentrated herds of elephants in the region ate up so much of the vegetation in the crucial corridor along the park's main river that nearly half of the area's eight hundred or so rhinos—an even more endangered species—died of starvation during the prevailing drought conditions.

In several of the elephant's last "strongholds" like Tsavo, the animal's huge appetites have pushed their environment to its limits under the crowding conditions that exist. Normally, this would be a natural process for the elephant and the environment. The elephants would feast heavily on a given area and then move to another area. While they were gone the first area would have the opportunity to regenerate itself.

However, today the herds are not so free to move on to new areas. They are hemmed in all sides by civilization, waiting poachers, and devastated lands. The pressure continues on the original parcel, preventing any significant regeneration. Some governments have come to the conclusion that certain numbers of elephants must be culled regularly to prevent damage to the environment from which it could

Cohesiveness in an elephant group involves several social factors, but the environmental aspects of water and food availability are most important.

An adult elephant fully digests less than half of the food it takes in and must therefore spend two-thirds of each day eating in order to meet its nutritional requirements.

never recover.

Like their African cousins, Asiatic elephants have a major impact on their environment. Their damages and destructions of trees open new clear areas within the jungles and forests, where lower growth can take hold and provide a new source of forage for the elephants and other herbaceous animals alike. Their constant use of the same trails throughout a region also maintains a network of "highways" of sorts for many creatures, including man. Some human roadways have actually been built along trails carved out by elephants.

The Diet and Digestion

Great volumes of food and water are required every day to power such a large frame. An elephant's digestive system makes full use of only forty percent of the nutrients that the animal consumes. To compensate for this low internal efficiency, the elephant spend nearly two-thirds of every day eating approximately three hundred to five hundred pounds of vegetation.

Grasses make up the bulk of the diet, but highly sought-after elephant delicacies include black plums, wild celery, and desert dates. In lean times, tree bark and similar rough vegetation will be eaten as well, and whole forests have been destroyed by herds of hungry elephants. Few edible items are out

An elephant rips inner bark from a felled baobab tree in Tsavo National Park, Kenya. Such a scene has been repeated countless times in a natural cycle that began when the first elephants inhabiting the ancient African forests encountered lean times.

*An aging baobab tree shows
the signs of bark shredding by
many generations of elephants.
Some naturalists today are
concerned about the ruinous
impact this habit poses on the
fragile African landscape.
Others see it as the inevitable
continuation of a practice that
existed before recorded time.*

of reach for the elephant. With that magnificent trunk, even the topmost branches of most trees can be ripped free and brought to the mouth. Fruit trees can be grasped with the trunk and shaken until they drop their bounty. Huge trees can be pushed, in bulldozer fashion, to the ground for leisurely munching.

And, those that can't be pushed over can be gouged with tusks and stripped of its bark. Baobab trees, with their very soft, liquid-filled inner bark, are a particular target for this. In some reserves, it is nearly impossible to find a baobab that has not been girdled by elephants. Still other elephants seem to prefer to dig for the tree roots with their trunks and front feet and then pry the roots from the ground. They have been observed spending a great deal of time in the pursuit of a single mouthful of tender root.

In like fashion, each adult elephant needs huge quantities of drinking water every day—on average, more than thirty gallons per elephant. Water sources are a major determinant of where the herds will wander and, for this reason, they are found over much larger ranges during the months of the rainy

A wooded area in the Samburu National Reserve, Kenya, shows the past ravages of a hungry herd of elephants. Few trees were spared. Although a leafy diet generally proves to be more nutritious and much easier to digest than one consisting of woody fibers, in times of drought and food shortage, the animals have few other alternatives.

Telltale tusk marks on this tree reveal that an elephant stripped the bark. The tree could most likely survive this one assault, but continued attacks by a herd of elephants could soon topple and destroy it.

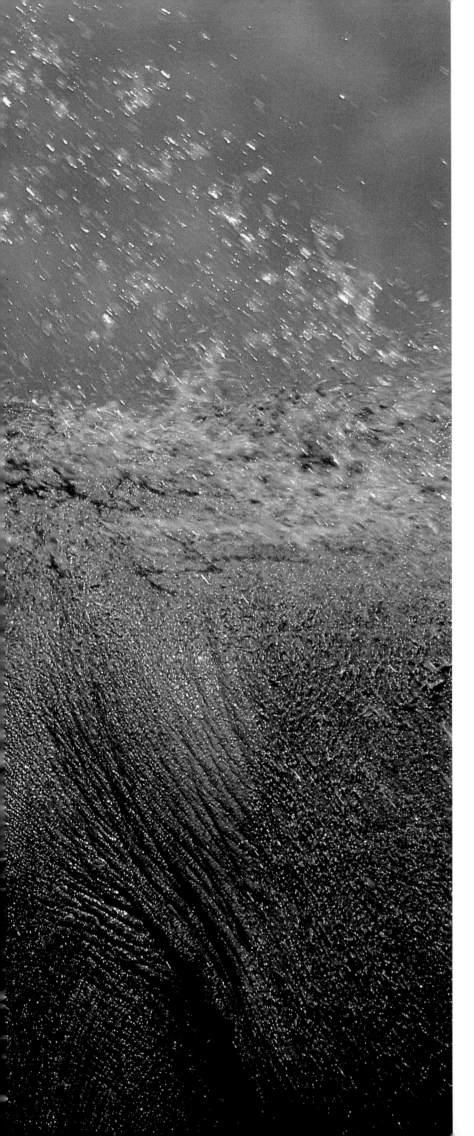

season.

Lakes and rivers provide the liquid in ample quantities at times, but often the animals are forced to dig their own wells, of sorts, in dry riverbeds. Scrapping with their front feet, they excavate large trenches until they reach the water that lies beneath. The entire herd will take advantage of the successful digger's good fortune, but only in their normal pecking order.

Water is vital to the everyday existence of the elephant. Not only does each individual need to drink large amounts of water daily, the liquid is used as one more means of cooling off. Filling its trunk from the nearest available source, the elephant showers the water across its ears. In particularly dry times, an elephant will even draw water from its own throat for use in this purpose. Several times each day the

Individual elephants consume huge amounts of vegetation daily. Full-grown adults, like this Indian bull elephant, may ingest as much as five hundred pounds in a twenty-four-hour period.

With a look of exuberance, an Indian elephant flings water across its back. Even the oldest and largest elephants sometimes appear to let go of their air of dignity when it comes to enjoying a water hole.

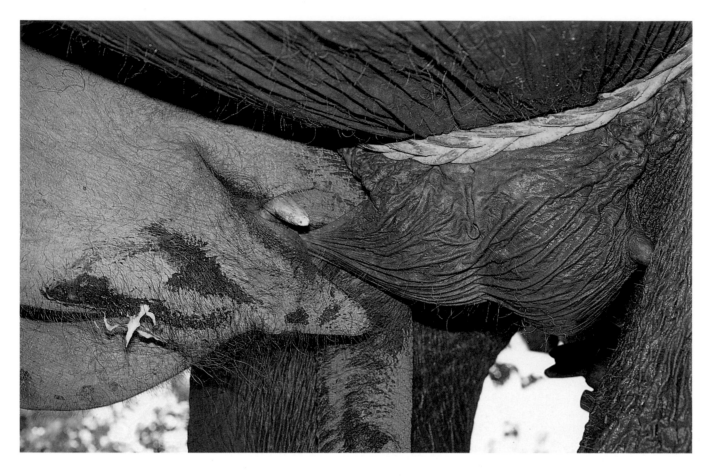

A baby suckles nourishment from its mother in Chiang Mai, Thailand. Several researchers have determined that the quality of the elephant's first-year diet plays an important role in determining how healthy the animal will be for the rest of its life.

The elephant must drink water at least once each day. More than a hundred quarts may be consumed by one pachyderm at a single stop.

Near the vast salt Etosha Pan in Namibia, a cow and her calf feed in the tall grass. The huge animals have terribly ineffective digestive systems and must spend about sixteen hours per day eating.

Elephants take great pleasure in bathing, as this Indian elephant reveals, often submerging themselves completely. They can remain underwater for surprisingly long periods of time, with only the tips of their trunks breaking the surface to take in air.

elephant will cease whatever activity it's engaged in to move to the nearest source of water for bathing and drinking.

Their drinking water and food generally supplies all of the elephants' needs for salt and other minerals. And they do show a definite preference for water that carries a high concentration of minerals. But salt licks and mineral licks are similarly cherished sites in elephant habitats. Elephants, along with many of the other animal species that inhabit the region, will repeatedly return to these sites to dig out and eat the earth. Deep trenches and even caves are often found in these spots, dug out by generations of pachyderms.

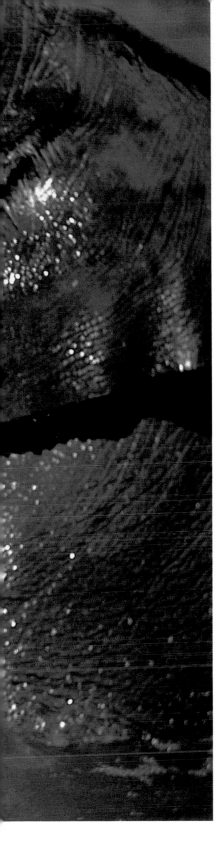

Hot and dry, a large bull Indian elephant hurries into the refreshing water. When water is in ample supply, all may share in drinking and bathing at the same time. However, a shortage will quickly cause the animals to observe their natural hierarchical order in satisfying their needs.

A small Indian elephant herd emerges from the forest at the edge of a river. The herd generally spends the morning at feeding grounds, but moves to water by midday, where it will stay for much of the afternoon. Nightfall will find them back at the feeding grounds.

African elephants have a deep attachment to the land. Not only do they take great pleasure in luxurious dust baths, they dig deep pits in search of salt and mineral licks.

These "wells" are used by virtually all other wildlife within the region. Some have been known to even hide their diggings under brush or even fill them in when leaving. If drought conditions become so severe that the elephants are forced to migrate to new range, the other creatures can suffer and even perish.

As a result of this great need for food and water, relatively large tracts of land are required for a healthy existence. These are commodities in great demand as man continues to overpopulate the planet, particularly in some of the areas shared with elephants. In turn, they are also commodities that bring the great animal increasingly into conflict with man—a struggle the elephant generally cannot win in the long run.

However, as the big animals travel they also transport the seeds for many different species of future

Members of a family await their turns to drink from a small underground water source. When water is extremely scarce, elephants will dig their own wells wherever they sense even minute quantities.

Putting their trunks to good use, a small group of elephants pause to refresh themselves at the edge of a water hole. Each one of the great beasts needs to hoist about thirty gallons of water to its mouth every day.

plants into new regions. Each adult elephant drops nearly two hundred pounds of manure each day, and only thirty to forty percent of that total is fully digested. To compensate for the low efficiency in food use, the elephant's system is able to handle enormous quantities of food very quickly. The small intestine is more than eighty feet in length, the appendix more than five feet, the large intestine more than twenty-one feet, and the rectum more than thirteen feet. This combined length is greater than the intestines of any other animal. The thundering stomach rumbles of the animal that are incumbent with such an extensive, fast-acting digestive system are legendary, although quite distinct from elephant language. Elephant digestive systems do much of the breaking down of food in the hindgut of the animal, meaning that elephants are prone to a great deal of flatulence.

Undigested food passes from the elephant much as it entered the animal, as nutrient-rich organic matter. This combination of high volume and low efficiency results in a great deal of available nutrients strewn about the landscape. It is left there as organic matter ready for use by other creatures.

Chief among these recyclers are the scarabs, a family (Scarabaeidae) of large beetles. Some are as large as six inches in length. Their appearance is marked by long horns growing from their heads, used by males in territorial combat. There are two primary groups of the scarabs, those that feed on fresh plant shoots and those that feed on decaying plants in animal manure, some of which specialize in elephant dung.

Several of the African species make use of elephant manure. A beetle digs into the balls of excrement to get at the softer, moister interior, from which it then rolls its own, much smaller balls. It then rolls the ball to a secure underground hiding place. Scarabs eat the dung, but they also use them as nurseries for their freshly hatched young. The male buries the ball of dung that it has constructed and the female then lays its eggs in the ball. When the young emerge from their eggs, they find themselves in the middle of a fantastic supply of food through which they must eat their way to freedom.

It is easy to attribute the emotion of joy to an elephant while watching it luxuriate in a bath—this Indian bull elephant certainly seems content. Although such human feelings cannot be definitively ascribed to animals, the pachyderm obviously derives some measure of pleasure and comfort from this activity.

All members of this group raise their trunks to relieve their thirst at an Etosha Pan water hole in Namibia. A full-grown adult is able to hoist several gallons at a time.

A spring-fed water hole in Chobe National Park, Botswana, serves as a daily magnet for many elephant herds. The activities of the elephant's day, year, and life are largely determined by the availability of water.

Two African elephants drink their fill in a wetland area of the Ngorongoro Crater in Tanzania. Calves learn to gather water in their trunks and deposit it into their mouths when they are about four months old. Until then, they kneel to drink with their mouths.

A small group of thirsty elephants converges on a water hole in Kenya. During drought conditions, such a group might travel many miles in search of water.

ORIGIN OF SPECIES

Only two representatives of the order Proboscidea remain today. They are the African elephant (*Loxodonta africana*), which inhabits areas of Africa south of the Sahara, and the Asiatic elephant (*Elephas maximus*), which is still found in India and portions of southeast Asia. The African elephant is further split into two major forms—savanna and forest—plus the hybrids that occur between the two.

The African species is the larger of the two, with some bulls standing as tall as thirteen feet at the shoulder and weighing more than fifteen thousand pounds. Indian bulls rarely reach ten feet in height and eleven thousand pounds in weight. Africa's version also has larger ears (as long as five feet from top to bottom) and more wrinkled skin; it is tallest at the shoulder, while the highest point on its Indian counterparts is the back. Both male and female African elephants grow tusks. In addition, the head of the African elephant is flat, while that of the Asiatic elephant is much more rounded.

The African Elephant

There are two subspecies of the African elephant: the forest elephant (*Loxodonta africana cyclotis*), which is bigger and has larger ears, and the savanna elephant (*Loxodonta africana oxyotis*). However, the two subspecies crossbreed quite readily, and many of the continent's elephants today carry some of both bloodlines.

A third, distinct "modern" subspecies, the Atlas elephant, had disappeared before any scientific studies could be done on it. It is believed that Hannibal's thirty-seven trained war elephants were of this subspecies. Records from such ancient civilizations as the Carthaginians in the region report the training of the Atlas elephant in the same way the Asiatic species is trained today.

African elephants inhabit nearly every type of habitat that their continent has to offer, excluding the desert regions. They are found everywhere from the swamps well up into the mountains.

A stand of trees can quickly take on the appearance of a heavily bombarded battlefield when a herd of elephants is confined there. Gnarled and broken stumps and scattered branches and limbs, denuded of all leaves, may be all that remain after an extended stay.

The Asiatic Elephant

Four distinct subspecies have been identified within the Asiatic species. They are the Indian elephant (*Elephas maximus bengalensis*), which are the postcard working elephants of India; the Malayan elephant (*Elephas maximus hirsutus*), which is the hairiest elephant alive today and also the most highly endangered; the Sumatran elephant (*Elephas maximus sumatranus*), which sports ears with four very straight edges and is also severely endangered; and the Ceylon elephant (*Elephas maximus maximus*), whose bulls have the lowest proportion of tusks of any elephant type.

Asiatic elephants inhabit nearly every habitat that southeast Asia offers and that has not been developed for man's uses. They are found in the tropical rainforests, the tall woodlands, the seemingly endless sea-jungles of tall grass, and even into the Himalayan Mountains.

The Pygmy Elephant

Through the millions of years of evolution there have been several miniature-size elephantlike species that arose and fell by the wayside. Some small individuals have also been recorded in more recent years, at times prompting the thought that perhaps they should be classified as a separate species or subspecies of pygmy elephants. One such "miniature" individual was discovered in the early 1900s, measuring just under six feet tall at the shoulders, although its age was determined to be six

The African elephant is the largest land animal on earth. A thirteen-foot, two-inch-tall bull, the most sizable specimen ever recorded, is on display in the entrance hall of the Smithsonian Institution in Washington, D.C.

The Indian elephant followed a somewhat different evolutionary path than its African relative. As a result, it is about one-third smaller and humpbacked rather than swaybacked. It also has a rounded rather than flat and sloping forehead, triangular ears, and a smoother trunk that has only one "finger" on its tip.

A lone bull feeds on aquatic plants in Kruger National Park, South Africa. Such plants are generally not as tender as the foliage that the elephant could pull from trees, yet in the dry season they may be all that's available.

The range of an elephant herd is dependent on available food and water. In some of the richer, lusher areas of Africa, the range may be no more than twenty square miles, while herds inhabiting the drier regions may travel over many hundreds of square miles.

years. Another, slightly larger individual was kept at the Bronx Zoo for several years.

Sightings of similarly small specimens continue today, however they are always of small individuals that are obviously adults and part of a grouping of otherwise normal-size animals. No herds of groupings made up entirely of miniatures have ever been reliably reported. These smaller animals are simply otherwise normal elephants with stunted growth, just as there are abnormally large elephants and unusually small and large specimens within all species of animals. They are not a distinct species.

Evolution and Ancestors

The two species of elephant that exist today, representing two different genera, evolved along a related but independent line from the mammoths and the mastodons. They are the sole remnants of a much more varied and widespread group that once roamed all continents of the earth, except for Antarctica and Australia. All told, more than three hundred different relatives of today's elephants have evolved and disappeared during the fifty-five million years that have passed since the first piglike *moeritherium* walked the earth.

The original design for today's two elephant types developed some five to fifteen million years ago in a species that has been named *Elephas primus*. Modern elephants are distantly related to the manatees and the rodentlike hyraxes of Africa. Although science came to understand the relationship

Most African elephants, as seen here, have tusks; but few female and only some male Asiatic elephants sport the elongated dentifrice. This is probably the result of the region's long history of hunting for ivory.

between these small tree and rock dwellers, native peoples in Africa have long referred to the hyraxes as the little brothers of the elephant.

They share a common original ancestor, a creature that more closely resembled a pig than it did any of its present-day de scendants. This animal originated in northern India during the Paleocene or Eocene epochs—fifty-five to sixty-five million years ago—the time frame in which most mammal families began.

As it sometimes does, evolution ran down many blind alleys from that original blueprint, giving the world a multitude of elephantlike species and orders that have no modern-day lineage.

A tapirlike creature, standing about two feet tall at the shoulder and weighing more than four

A Burchell's zebra decides to concede the area after a head-shaking, trumpeting display by an elephant. However, the threat approach was almost certainly a bluffing tactic, as elephants have very little incentive to take any real action against other grazing animals.

An African elephant passes by a black rhinoceros—a sight that is likely to become increasingly rare in just a few years. Both animals are endangered, yet continue to be stalked by poachers.

hundred pounds, the moeritherium roamed the swamps of northern Africa until the Oligocene epoch, about thirty-eight million years ago. At the same time, another branch of the family tree was producing the *phiomia* in Africa. This animal more closely resembled today's elephant, standing about nine feet tall and sporting the rudimentary beginnings of a short trunk. This species also disappeared before the Miocene epoch, twenty-five million years ago.

The *deinotherium* inhabited southern Europe, Africa, and India from the Miocene epoch, twenty-five million years ago, until the beginnings of the Pleistocene epoch, two million years ago. It looked much like modern African elephants, but with walruslike tusks protruding down into backward curls from the lower jaw. A four-tusked—two from the top jaw and two from the bottom—group of elephant ancestors emerged in Africa, Asia, Europe, and North America at about the same time. Most members of this group stood about ten feet tall at the shoulder.

African nations have begun to recognize the elephant as a major factor for tourism. Entire industries are growing around the huge mammals, such as sightseeing from hot-air balloons.

In their constant search for huge amounts of vegetation and water, elephants travel great distances and occasionally do "invade" human agricultural areas. It is generally the elephants who suffer most from such confrontations. Persistent marauders are often killed for their transgressions.

The first record of human beings taming elephants for their own use dates to about 3500 B.C. Over the centuries they have been trained for performance; heavy, bulldozerlike work; transportation; hunting; and warfare.

By bathing his elephant, an Indian mahout builds and maintains his close relationship with the animal. This practice draws upon the elephant's own social customs, which involve a great deal of touching and stroking.

An Indian mahout leads his shackled elephant to a water hole to allow the working animal to drink.

During the late Miocene Period, several strange shovel-tusked elephants species developed in Europe, Africa, and Asia (the *platybelodons*) and in North America (the *amebelodons*). In place of the rounded, pointed tusks that we associate with modern elephants, these ten-foot-tall animals carried flattened, wider ivory that protruded from the lower jaw like two shovel blades. These specialized apparatus adapted the animals to a life of dredging aquatic plants from the bottoms of rivers, lakes, and swamps.

In the category of strange tusks we must place the *cuviero nius*, which sported a pair of ivories, each one twisted in spirals like the horn of the fabled unicorn. The nine-foot-tall elephant first evolved in North America during the late Miocene, perhaps six to eight million years ago. Herds found their way into South America just a couple of million years ago. The last remnants of the species survived there until about A.D. 400. Man's hunting for was probably the reason for the demise of these last cuvieronius.

The "hairy elephants" we know as the mammoths are another group that evolved relatively recently: less than two million years ago. The nine-foot-tall woolly mammoth

Young Indians bathe an equally young elephant in the Kabinin River, India. The mahouts, who train and work the elephants, often involve their entire families in the business and the caretaking of the animals.

(*Mammuthus primigenius*) of North America, Europe, and Asia, with its forward-protruding recurved tusks, is the image that commonly comes to mind. The lesser-known *Mammuthus trogontherii* was the largest elephantlike creature ever to roam the earth. This European species towered at more than fifteen feet at the shoulder and carried a pair of tusks that could extend more than seventeen feet in length.

With their heavy coats of fur, the mammoths were adapted to life in cold climates. As the glaciers receded, the mammoths followed in a northward direction. The last of their kind lived until less than ten thousand years ago. The general warming of the earth's atmosphere and subsequently changing habitat were primary factors in their demise. But early man killed plenty of the great beasts as well, probably speeding the species' extinction.

Tourists in Corbett National Park, India, take in the sights from the back of a safari-trained elephant. Indian elephants are still domesticated and made to do heavy labor in many parts of their range. The practice dates back more than five centuries.

Many complete specimens have been found fully preserved in ice. Small bits of DNA have been recovered from some of them. Rumors persistently come out of the villages of the northlands of shaggy mammoths that have been spotted alive, although none have been proven true.

The word "mastodon" is commonly used as a synonym for mammoth, although the mastodons were actually earlier relatives that occurred as early as the Oligocene, twenty-five to thirty-eight million

Herds of elephants and hippopotami share a portion of the Savuti Channel in Chobe National Park, Botswana. Encounters between the two species are not always so cordial.

A caravan of elephant-borne tourists moves makes its way through Chitwan National Park in Nepal. The tourism dollars that the big creatures can attract into such poor nations may well play a major role in the ultimate salvation of the elephant in the wild.

A water hole at Etosha Pan in Namibia reflects the impressive image of a large African elephant.

years ago. They shared the woolly coat of the mammoths, but were smaller—the largest stood no more than ten feet at the shoulder—and had nonmammoth, modern elephant tuberculate teeth. The last of the mastodons, a species known as *stegomastodon*, survived until about one million years ago in North America and slightly more recently in South America.

Modern elephants emerged from the same family Elephantidae as did the mammoths, some miniature island-dwelling species, and a few woodland species. Only the African and Indian types are still with us, the descendants of species that evolved to occupy a niche in the warmer, more southerly climates.

One of the reasons that today's existing elephant species survived while other, quite similar species fell by the wayside can be found in the animal's teeth. Many of those other elephantlike species, such as the mastodons, were equipped with low-crowned, smooth-surfaced teeth adapted for a vegetarian diet and grinding in a sideways motion. On the other hand, the direct ancestors of today's elephants sported teeth with elevated crowns and strong ridges adapted to tearing and pulverizing as the ridges meet. This was crucial to survival, as the available vegetation changed and a new grassland environment replaced the more forested surroundings of previous times.

A trio of tuskers grazes at the base of a tree in a Kenyan game reserve, Kenya. There is evidence of intensive browsing and damage to the tree's branches.

Creating an otherworldly scenario, a lone African elephant moves past a swamp at sunset.

ELEPHANT SOCIETY

Elephants exist in a highly structured, tightly knit, matriarchal world. Families that do not show the unnatural impact of poaching generally consist of a dozen or more related elephants that are led by one mature female. Such groups are increasingly difficult to find under modern, manmade circumstances. The family bond runs through the ties of the old female and her female descendants. Every generation of female from grandmother to newborn grandchild may be found in one herd.

Bulls, on the other hand, are generally forced to leave the herd when they reach puberty, at about age twelve. After a young bull has been driven out from his mother's group, he will remain as close by as the members of the group will permit for many days. Eventually, he will come into contact with a group of bulls, which he will join. All-male groups are generally found in close vicinity to the female family units, although mating and times of severe danger are the only instances when they will come into direct contact.

This matriarchal society is a relatively recent discovery about the elephant. It emerged only after researchers began supplying most of our knowledge about the animals; previously, we had relied on reports of hunters and adventurers, who had believed that each group of elephants was led by a dominant male. In defense of the latter, an elephant's sex can be difficult to determine at a distance. The sex organs are not prominent and generally hidden by folds of skin, and both sexes have tusks. But this example of such crucial knowledge gained in only the past quarter-century illustrates how very little we still really know about these animals.

Family Groups

The family groups may join into herds with other family groups, often with some shared lineage, in the same general area. When any of the groups within a clan happen to meet in their daily wanderings, there is much excitement that seems best described in terms of a family reunion. They actually rush toward each other, filling the air with their elephant voices.

The size of such herds is highly variable, although it tends toward much smaller numbers than it once did as a result of modern pressures from man. Still it remains that in times of plenty of food and water, the herds will be much larger than in lean times. Under extreme hardship conditions, even the family groups may splinter into smaller collections. In areas of plentiful food and water, an elephant herd might remain within a home range of only a couple dozen square miles

Heedless of distant stormy skies, a herd of African elephants makes its way across a game reserve in Kenya.

A large herd of elephants in Amboseli National Park, Kenya, appears to be much closer than it actually is to Mount Kilimanjaro, the tallest mountain in Africa. The snow-capped peaks, which rise 19,340 feet above sea level, are in reality several miles distant.

When well fed and free of most threats, family groups—including even the lead matriarch—engage in much playful activity. Observers agree that the word silly is probably the most apt description.

throughout the year. However, when either commodity becomes scarce, that range might extend over many hundred square miles.

This society is maintained through a highly tactile lifestyle, centered on that versatile trunk. The sense of smell plays a crucial role in the social life of the elephant. The greeting ritual among individuals begins with a mutual touching with the trunks of each other's glands on the cheeks and temples, and then in the genital areas. Mother and baby spend a great deal of time caressing one another. Family members interrupt activities throughout the day to engage in gently touching one another. Members of groups passing one another in the African brush will pause to exchange touches. Although they generally do not follow any elaborate courting rituals, a bull courting a cow may intertwine his trunk with hers. Even a dead carcass left by poachers will be poked and probed at length by every passing elephant. Bulls often engage in mock battles, sparring with their trunks rather than their tusks.

"An elephant never forgets," we've been told time and time again, and the fabled memory of the great beasts does seem to have some basis in truth. Field research has found that an adult elephant is able to recognize every member of its family grouping— and extended groupings of even larger numbers—as individuals. Similarly, water holes and prime feeding locations across the animal's great range are recalled with ease, even when they were last visited several months or even years earlier.

Grief and Other Emotions

To witness the death of a female elephant in a herd of its family and relations, even for the most

Elephant society is very much a matriarchal existence. A lead cow heads the group, which is generally comprised of her offspring. Several such groups may unite into a herd, organized along the bloodlines of their lead females.

Including members of several generations, a herd of elephants crosses a Kenyan river. Such groups are led by females and composed of female relatives and their offspring.

A huge herd of elephants, accompanied by flocks of cattle egrets, stretches out across a wetland in the South Sudan.

hard-bitten scientist, is to become a believer in the ability of these great animals to feel emotions. When the dying animal first falls to its knees or onto its sides, other members of the herd will immediately form the traditional circle of protection around it. After a bit, sensing no external threats to the rest of the group, they will push their fallen comrade and try to help her back onto its feet.

After much of this effort, and only after not a single bit of life can be sensed in the dead elephant, the herd will begin to feed nearby. But there will be a restless, uneasy feeling about their every action for the rest of the day. Eventually, every member of the group will return at one point or another to stand over the body. Some, apparently with greater ties to the fallen individual, will linger much longer than the others. All will touch their former comrade with their trunks. As darkness brings its close to the day, they will leave the body.

While the body decomposes and its flesh is reclaimed by the earth over the next several weeks and months, any elephant that passes within scenting range is likely to divert its path to move near the carcass and to touch it. And, for years to come, elephants chancing upon the sun-bleached remains will stop to carefully examine the bones in a strange silence. To many observers all this grief and mourning comes amazingly close to the emotions that pour out at some of man's own viewings, such as at funerals and cemeteries.

Long-term observers have verified as a fact the tendency of individual elephants to exhibit their own special moods, emotions, likes, and dislikes—an individual personality, if you will. This extends to the interactions with other members of their group and members of other groups. Each elephant seems to have those other elephants that it likes, those that it dislikes, and those toward which it feels little emotion one way or the other. These emotions regularly manifest themselves in outward demonstration, such as the bullying of a disliked individual.

Domesticated Indian elephant cows spend some leisure time after work beside the Manas River, India.

Raising the Young

Most members of a family grouping share in the various duties of rearing a young elephant, sometimes beginning with the birth. Although some cows simply go off on their own and later return with their newborn, others—particularly first-time mothers—receive significant assistance from the comrades. They might help pull the newborn from the mother in a particularly difficult birth, remove the fetal membrane from around the baby, and help it to get to its feet. Twins are an extremely rare occurrence in elephants. Only a few instances have been reliably recorded since man began studying the

A group of elephants pauses to observe a passing herd of buffalo at the Caterpillar Pan in Hwange National Park, Zimbabwe.

Bulls move from one group to another, seeking cows in estrus with which to mate. The bulls form no lasting relationships with any of these groups and generally stay with any one of them for no more than a few days.

In both Africa and Asia, loss of habitat poses as great a threat to the remaining wild elephant populations as does the poacher's rifle.

Family portrait, from right to left: mother, baby, and older sibling. The baby is attempting to pilfer food from its sister's mouth. It may also pick up any scraps that fall from the mouths of its family while they eat.

The greeting ceremony, as does much of the elephant's existence, centers on the trunk and involves touching and intertwining, as these two Indian elephants show.

great beasts.

For as long as the first six months of life, the baby suckles with its mouth. But once it has learned to use its trunk—something it must learn about drinking water as well—the infant will turn to this more convenient instrument. Elephant babies are born weighing between 250 and 270 pounds and standing about three feet tall at the shoulder. They need about ten quarts of mother's milk every day.

Between two and three years of age, they begin to grow their tusks. Shortly thereafter, those elongated teeth will cause the cow discomfort when the infant attempts to nurse and the weaning process begins. Some cows, however, show much more tolerance than others, allowing the calf to nurse for several more years, even after she has carried and given birth to a new infant. The siblings will be seen nursing together.

As big as they are, young elephant calves are regularly lifted off the ground and over obstacles in their mothers' trunks. Such lifting begins soon after the youngster has entered the world as part of the mother's becoming familiar with her new charge. Others in the group may also lift the youngster.

Although it may continue to nurse on mother's milk for several years, the young elephant is able to handle solid food within a few weeks of birth. It is not yet ready to chew the vegetation, however, and older members readily help it with this task. They will rip the vegetation from the tree or ground, clear it of all nonedibles, and chew it into very small pieces before offering it to the youngster. In time,

A baby elephant holds out its trunk in greeting other members of the family group. The action is instinctive even in newborn calves and integral to the social fabric of the herd.

Regular dust baths help these elephants control insects and other pests, as well as provide a screening effect against the intense rays of the Namibian sun.

Two young elephants nuzzle each other after quenching their thirst at an Etosha Pan water hole in Namibia.

The social, caring structure of the elephant grouping extends to all members of the herd, which generally includes a few females that are often related and subsequent generations of females. Only the very young males are tolerated within the group for any length of time.

the infant comes to help itself by reaching into the mouths of the adults even when nothing has been offered to it. This action is not tolerated by all adults nor in older youngsters.

A baby elephant might stay at its mother's side for as long as fifteen years. Even after that age, a female is likely to remain with her mother's family grouping. Babysitting for the group's several youngsters that no longer need to remain as constantly closely to their mothers is a duty that passes among the various members of the group. The matriarch of the group and sometimes other more dominant members often do not take their turns in this chore. It is most often assigned by chance to the cow that finds herself to be the last one leaving the water hole, which generally is still engaging the youngsters. Young elephants will spend endless amounts of time at play in the water and generally need to be forced from the water.

As touchingly tender as the other members of the herd are with their calves, there do seem to be some limits. Water—or more precisely, the shortage of water—is one such instance. When a mother is forced to dig a well to get at the water and junior crowds in to drink first, sometimes collapsing the sides of the hole, she will push the youngster back to wait his turn.

However, under the most threatening of circumstances, most cows seem unerringly faithful to their calves. When a calf dies, its mother and others in the family grouping may spend days trying to get it back on its feet. Some mothers have been observed carrying the dead body about on their tusks for

The wild African elephant can live to be more than sixty years old, yet only the most protected of these big mammals can be expected to live out their full natural life spans today.

The herd generally will not abandon an injured member. Instead, members will try to nudge their comrade back onto its feet with their tusks and help the wounded elephant maintain its footing.

Most wild elephant herds are now confined to designated parks and preserves that are much more restricted than the animals' original ranges. As a result, the herds' diet is restricted and birthrates have declined, by as much as half in some locales.

A young bull is permitted to remain with its mother's group until reaching
puberty, at about twelve years old. The bull may attempt to stay with the herd
for a considerable time thereafter, following as close as the group will allow.
Eventually, though, it will join a group consisting only of bulls.

several days.

Under severe drought conditions that wear on for long periods, this devotion can have disastrous results. The youngsters are generally the first to die off at these times, but they are often joined in death by their mothers who are unwilling to abandon their fallen offspring.

Lions and hyenas are among the primary predators on very young elephants. Most often they pick up the calves that are sick or injured or for some other reason lags behind the protection of the family grouping. A healthy calf generally remains out of reach for these animals. Also, sometimes the would-be predator ends up impaled on a tusk or smashed underfoot or chased into the safety of a nearby tree.

This is not to say that elephant meat is not on the menu for animals like lions and hyenas. Many of the hunting species will feast on a carcass left by poachers or felled by some more natural cause. It is not uncommon to find a pride of lions or a pack of hyenas in the vicinity of a dead elephant. Lions seem to be a particular target of much of the elephant's aggression. More than a few cubs have been caught too far from the nearest trees and trampled to death by a group of elephants. Popular lore often reports this as vengeance on the part of the elephants for their own young killed by lions, but it is actually rooted in a general attitude that all African elephants carry toward all lions.

Bull Confrontations

The classic bone-crunching, flesh-ripping battles between bull elephants that are standard fare of early jungle movies are extremely rare in the wild. The bulls generally exist within a hierarchy that has been established for many years. More often than not, the entire affair consists of nothing more than a few key signals of body language.

Unlike the males of so many other animal species, bull elephants do not stake out and defend territories. Only when two bulls that are unfamiliar with one another or of nearly equal stature claim a cow in estrus will true battles over any sort of "territory" occur.

Battles most often take place among younger bulls who must establish and maintain their positions within the male hierarchy of a region. Older, more mature bulls rarely need to engage in direct physical contact. Even the squabbles among the younger bulls are generally short-lived affairs, with the lesser bull soon learning of his disadvantage and giving ground to his superior. In these mock battles, the two young bulls run at each other with their trunks extended over their foreheads. Before they collide, their trunks touch and entwine. From that point on, it's a shoving match, with each one trying to force the other backward. If they are closely matched in strength and agility, and neither one budges, both

A baby Indian elephant plays with vegetation that floated by during its bath. The young elephant is intensely curious about and exploratory toward its environment.

A seasonal abundance of water and food gives the elephant a temporary respite to prepare for more stressful periods. This is also a time of much play and mock battles among the young.

Two youngsters butt heads during play at the Samburu National Reserve, Kenya. During periods of ample food and water, the elephant's first ten to twelve years of life can be largely carefree and playful.

will back off. After a few minutes, they will rush each other again and begin the whole affair anew.

In those rare instances where a real battle breaks out, the two bulls go through with their charge. Their tusks clash, their foreheads butt severely, and their trunks intertwine much more forcefully. Tusks are occasionally broken under these impacts, and sometimes bodies are penetrated and deaths result.

Mating and Birth

Bulls generally initiate the mating process by approaching a group of females and beginning to examine individuals. A bull testing a cow that otherwise seems receptive to his mating advances will touch the tip of his trunk to her genital area and then place it into his mouth. He will do this repeatedly until he is satisfied about her state of readiness.

Receptive females, in addition to exuding the various smells associated with estrus, demonstrate their readiness by backing their rear ends into the face of the bull. He, in turn, place his extended trunk along her back and pushes forward with his tusks.

At this point, if the female chooses to accept his advances, she trots off from the group. The bull follows closely. She slows to a walk that takes her in his general direction, and he hurries to cut her off. When their paths meet, if she has fully accepted him, they will intertwine their trunks. This courtship sparring process is repeated several times, until the female begins presenting her back end to the male

An elephant cow usually gives birth to a single calf. Twins emerge in about one in one hundred births, and survival of both is rare. Triplets have been reliably reported.

A female African elephant carries a developing fetus for about twenty-two months. When the gestation is over, the mother gives birth to nearly 260 pounds of baby that will suckle two to three gallons of milk every day for the next five or six years.

more frequently.

The end of the "dance" comes when the cow stops, falls to her knees and hoists her tail. Again the male touches the tip of his trunk to her vagina. The next repetition will result in the bull mounting the cow and very briefly inserting his penis. Bulls encountering reluctant females will sometimes attempt to force them into this activity, singling them out from the group and pushing them. This usually does not result in copulation.

The cow generally becomes pregnant for the first time at about the age of ten. Nearly all females are generally mated by their eighteenth year. From that point, she is able to produce young throughout her life. A female that escapes the poachers and lives out a normal life of sixty or so years may give birth to an average of seven offspring. Less than three-quarters of her offspring will live to become adults.

Many females enter their estrus periods during the wet season, which can occur from November through May. This coincides with the time of greatest concentration in large herds, a period when mating opportunities are at their greatest. Conception during this period, followed by a gestation period of about twenty-two months, also tends to produce babies at that time of the year when food and water are at their most plentiful.

The gestation period extends for about twenty-two months, at the end of which a single calf is usually

Calves begin feeding on vegetation, in combination with their mothers' milk, at about four months. After approximately six months, their diet includes a large portion of vegetation.

With baby in tow, a cow African elephant lumbers across the bushland, languid and unhurried. The calf never strays more than a few feet away from its mother during its first year of life.

Elephants, both Indian like these and African, are much better swimmers than their huge bulk would seem to indicate. Although they prefer to walk through the water, rivers and small lakes that are too deep for wading offer virtually no impedance to a group that really wants to get to the other side.

After a bracing mud bath, this small elephant calf enjoys a few gallons of mother's milk. Babies will attempt, and be allowed, to suckle from all or most females in the group, although they are most likely to find success with their mothers.

born. In an uncomplicated, healthy birth, the calf's head emerges first. The 250-pound newborn will suckle two to three gallons of mother's milk each day during its first few weeks of life. Each cow has only two teats. Unlike most animals, these teats are located between her forelegs. It will be three to six years before the infant is completely weaned. By this point, the young elephant will have doubled its size.

Although truly old elephants are quite rare today, the offspring—under natural conditions without any involvement from man—might expect to live more than sixty years. It would be nearly full grown at about the midway point.

Musth

Musth, a period in bulls that ranges from a few days to a few months at a time, is generally marked by extremely aggressive behavior toward just about everything in their immediate vicinity. When a working elephant enters this period, its mahout secures it tightly to trees until the condition passes.

During musth, glands at the cheek and temple of the bull secrete a foul-smelling liquid that can be seen on the animal's face from quite a distance and resembles streams of dark tears. Although elephants are generally nonterritorial in relation to geography, a bull in musth mark trees throughout its range with this liquid by rubbing its forehead and face on them.

Musth seems to play some role in mating, and bulls in this condition

Except for human beings, adult elephants have no natural enemies and are well equipped to defend themselves against all other animals—including the hippopotamus, as shown here. The big cats do, however, prey upon baby elephants.

Raw ivory currently sells for more than fifty dollars per pound, an amazing increase from two to three dollars per pound, the rate it brought as recently as the mid-1960s. The average tusk of an African elephant weighs about fourteen pounds, which means that a single pair of tusks is worth far more than the total annual income of most people living near the remaining herds.

After a refreshing drink, two young African bulls exchange traditional elephant greetings by intertwining their trunks. When such bonding occurs between a male and female, it often signals the start of courtship, prior to mating.

The act of mating generally lasts less than a minute for elephants. Some males stay with the females for several hours afterward, while others leave much sooner in search of other females in estrus.

seems to be more active in their pursuit of cows; however, nonmusth bulls are regularly observed engaged in the activity as well. This strange condition appears to occur at any time, although the more dominant bulls seem to enter it at those months of the year when most females within their region are ready for sexual advances.

A strange aspect of the musth condition was thought to be a disease when it was first observed in the early 1980s by researchers Joyce Poole and Cynthia Moss. They initially labeled what they saw as "green penis syndrome." Additional observation, however, revealed that it was actually caused by the nonstop dribbling of urine by a male in musth.

The condition of musth more than likely is the root cause of the infamous "rogue elephant," so common in the many jungle movies seen on late-night television but much less so in real life. Extreme cases of the condition have brought individual elephants to the brink of madness, which could be directed at humans that happen to occupy the general vicinity of the animal. Even ancient carvings report on the necessity to kill rampaging elephants from time to time.

Sleeping

Observations of elephants in recent years have also led to new findings in other areas. Contrary to previous ideas about the elephant, they do lie down to sleep—younger ones for longer periods than fully mature adults. As they seem to do this more in the middle of the night and are quick to get to their feet at the slightest disturbance, the practice went unobserved in the wild for quite some time. In

Two young bulls in a Kenyan game reserve spar to test their dominance over one another. Such fights generally end without serious injury to either party.

Tussles like this between two Namibian-dwelling bulls generally end without any real harm to either combatant. However, both animals have the power and the tools necessary to do mortal damage to their foe.

The nearer of these two African bulls is almost on his knees during a shoving match to test dominance. The more powerful males in a given range tend to engage in most of the mating with females in estrus.

Testing their respective places in the dominance hierarchy, two bulls shove at each other after leaving a water hole at Etosha Pan, Namibia.

addition, most will also doze for brief periods while standing. More recent observations have found that some of them even fashion crude pillows for themselves of whatever soft vegetation is close at hand. Calves, which already spend a great deal of time together in the group's "kindergarten," often lean against one another to sleep.

Adult elephants do not need much sleep, no more than five hours per night, which they generally take on their feet. It is not a very deep sleep and is interrupted at intervals of less than thirty minutes for inspection of the animal's surroundings for any sign of danger. Infants tend to sleep many more hours and much more frequently during both day and night.

In a herd of elephants, not every member will sleep at the same time. Most will be dozing in the wee hours of the morning, but generally at least one of their number will have "drawn" guard duty and remains alert.

Communicating

The few that do not sleep will probably communicate softly through a system of interaction that is only beginning to be understood. Grunts, trumpets, rumbles, screeches, and sounds that are below the range of human hearing combine with a great deal of body language to form the elephant's communication system—a system that human researchers are only begin-

ning to understand. Until very recently many of the sounds were interpreted as nothing more than the rumblings of the constantly hungry pachyderms' stomachs.

Katharine Payne and William Langbauer, wildlife biologists at Cornell University in Ithaca, New York, have recently uncovered the ability of African elephants to generate low-frequency sound by forcing air through their nasal passages. These ultralow sounds are generated deep in the elephant's throat, but make use of the long passages in the animal's trunk and other body cavities as amplifiers.

Payne first discovered the low sounds coming from elephants at the Washington Park Zoo in Portland, Oregon. On a hunch, based on years of whale communication research, she recorded several hours of what was silence to the human ear in the vicinity of the elephants. When she played the tape at a different speed, it was alive with elephant vocalizations.

Among the reasons behind the few vocalizations that have been deciphered thus far are a female's openness to advances from a potential mate, excitement on reunion with a familiar group, and coordination of movements among different groups. Observers of trained Asiatic elephants have reported that the animals also "bubble contentedly" in anticipation of supper when returning from a day afield.

A female elephant gives birth on an average of once every four or five years. Her previous calf, if still alive, has continued to suckle throughout the intervening years.

A dust-kicking tussle between two of its larger, more dominant members sends the rest of the herd in search of a more peaceful setting in Amboseli National Park, Kenya.

A temporal gland, which secretes a thick fluid, is located behind each of the elephant's eyes. The drainage from this gland becomes much more pronounced in males that have entered musth, the period when they are primed for mating.

A giraffe becomes uneasy and decides to move to more neutral territory as a trio of elephants wallows in a nearby mud hole.

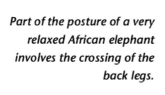

Part of the posture of a very relaxed African elephant involves the crossing of the back legs.

A herd of African elephants forms the defensive circular position that is so effective against natural enemies, yet so useless in the face of poachers' rifles.

A bull kicks up a cloud of dust as it halts a short, bellowing charge in Timbavati, South Africa. Although this is the Hollywood image of the elephant, the big animal is generally more inclined to a peaceful existence.

Subsequent experiments in Etosha National Park in Namibia have demonstrated that elephants respond in different ways to variations on these sounds, which can be picked up by the big animals at least two-and-a-half miles distant.

The rumbling sounds are most often produced among groups of elephants and have rarely been heard coming from isolated, solitary animals. Some researchers believe these long-carrying sounds might provide the explanation for the apparently coordinated movements they have observed in elephant groups that were beyond sight of one another.

Trumpeting—the more familiar elephant sound—is generally associated with excitement: when threatened, when charging or staging the more likely fake charge, when separated from the family grouping, or when exuberant on greeting an old acquaintance. It appears that trumpeting is more an outward expression of strong emotions, while the little-understood rumblings serve the basic communications needs of the animals.

Defense Tactics

A means of defense that the typical herd of elephants commonly employs is to form a circle of their bodies, with the adults facing outward against the threat and the young animals protected inside the ring. The adults than raise the trunks and tusks to display their potential weapons. They flex their ears to their maximum extension. Some may charge the perceived source of danger in what usually

An immense bull African elephant is startled by the passing of a tiny steenbok, a plains antelope. The huge pachyderms do not always seem totally cognizant of the advantage their size poses.

One member of a small herd of African elephants reacts to the photographer's presence by suddenly adopting a cautious, warning posture.

Elephants experiencing prolonged stress and environmental threats tend to congregate in much larger groups than would be natural in the wild.

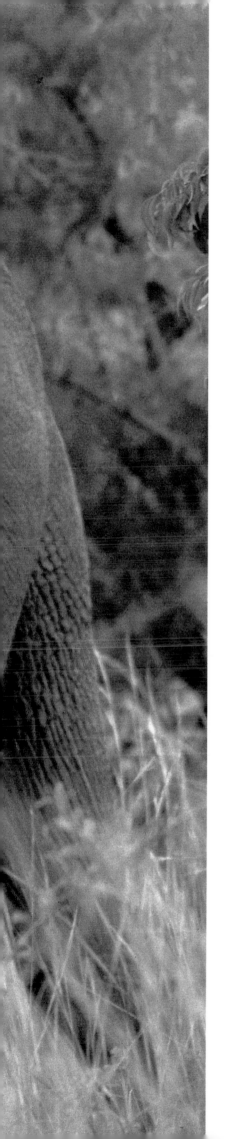

After a refreshing drink and bath, two African elephants share a calm moment at the river's edge. One is obviously more relaxed than its companion.

An elephant herd runs through the brushy countryside in Etosha National Park, Namibia. Such panicked runs are generally short-lived, unless the source of the scare continues to frighten the elephants.

With ears raised and held erect, a Kenyan bull registers alarm. This is either an instinctive action or one that is learned very early in life, because even the baby elephant enters into the threat display when an intruder approaches unexpectedly.

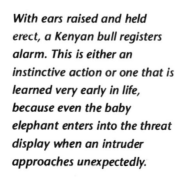

Like shadowy beings from another age, two hulking figures move through the Linyanti Swamp in Botswana after filling up on water for the night.

amounts to nothing more than mock attacks. All this show is generally more than enough to back off any natural enemy that temporarily forgot the status of the elephants in their environment.

As effective as such maneuvers might be against any of the few natural enemies within the elephant's natural world, such defense is useless against armed poachers. This method of defense has also spelled disaster for more than one family group faced with advancing brush fires. The elephants view the fires as they would any other threat, but their circle serves only to entrap them in the flames.

At other times, possibly much more commonly under today's threatened circumstances, the entire herd will erupt into a ground-thundering stampede over everything in their path. Such headlong dashes have been reported to go on for more than thirty minutes, carrying the herd over considerable distance, before the alarm dissipates.

Hunters' and adventurers' accounts by the hundreds have told us in graphic detail of deadly charges by massive bull elephants that ended in one last-minute, life-saving shot from a high-powered rifle. But observers who have spent a great deal of time around elephants know that a simple clap of the

Elephant calves are able to walk and stay with their group immediately upon birth. In all other aspects of life and livelihood, however, they are completely dependent on the group.

A thick fog rises off the Linyanti Swamp in Botswana, enveloping a quartet of passing elephants in the orange sunset.

In the early twentieth century, more than one hundred thousand elephants were killed every year, according to some estimates. Their ivory tusks were in demand as the raw material for pool balls and piano keys. Near the middle of the century, the commercial demand waned, as did much of the slaughter—only to see a resurgence in recent decades.

Nightfall comes to Kazaranga National Park, India, as a solitary elephant feeds from the stack of grasses provided by its handler.

hands is generally enough to put a halt to the charge and send the elephant running into the brush.

Hair-raising depictions of the fierce attack of an elephant continued well into recent times. Descriptions such as the fol lowing from a 1954 book by Oskar Koenig were not at all uncommon among adventurers and hunters from the period: "The elephant's attack is annihilating in its fury and power. He hates man, who for hundreds of years has hunted him for the ivory in his tusks." However, adult elephants rarely "throw their weight around" in attempts at bullying other animals. As a matter of fact, even large bulls often decide to simply vacate an area when some much lesser creatures cause a ruckus.

Young individuals, however, are another story entirely. Elephants youngsters do have their many frisky moments and, at those times, any seemingly vulnerable creature in the immediate vicinity might become a target for the animal's fake charges.

What many observers have described as a heart-stopping charge—ears flapping, trunk lifted overhead—is actually an exploratory position. This is a typical posture of curiosity. The elephant is attempting to get a fix on its surroundings and whatever is causing its concern. If it were charging, its ears would be held back against the head, its trunk would be guarded back at its chest, and its head would be lowered.

Contrary to folklore, elephants are not afraid of mice in the least. There is no way that a mouse could run up an elephant's trunk unless the pachyderm allowed it. Experiments with captive animals have found that the elephant first inspects the mouse by smelling it and then quickly loses interest in the minuscule creature. However, those same experiments found that elephants exhibited an unexplainable apprehension about being close to rabbits.

Before the twentieth century, there were more than ten million elephants in Africa. Optimistic estimates place the current total at less than eight hundred thousand, and pessimistic projections see at least eighty thousand being killed each year.

Although the elephant graveyard is a myth, it is a myth based on some reality. Sick and injured elephants do sometimes move into areas where food and water are plentiful, such as near a lake, and eventually die there. It is probable that several elephants might choose a particularly suitable site for this same need and, through their deaths over time, amass a number of skeletons in a relatively limited area.